MIND YOUR MANNERS

a witty guide

MIND YOUR MANNERS

a witty guide

Judith Martin
Nicholas Ivor Martin

Viva Books

New Delhi | Mumbai | Chennai | Kolkata | Bengaluru | Hyderabad | Kochi | Guwahati

First Indian Edition 2014
Reprinted 2015, 2017, 2019

VIVA BOOKS PRIVATE LIMITED

- 4737/23 Ansari Road, Daryaganj, New Delhi 110 002
  E-mail: vivadelhi@vivagroupindia.net, Tel. 42242200
- 76, Service Industries, Shirvane, Sector 1, Nerul, Navi Mumbai 400 706
  E-mail: vivamumbai@vivagroupindia.net, Tel. 27721273, 27721274
- Megh Tower, Old No. 307, New No. 165, Poonamallee High Road, Maduravoyal
  Chennai 600 095 E-mail: vivachennai@vivagroupindia.net, Tel. 23780991, 23780992
- B-103, Jindal Towers, 21/1A/3 Darga Road, Kolkata 700 017
  E-mail: vivakolkata@vivagroupindia.net, Tel. 22836381, 22816713
- 7, Sovereign Park Apartments, 56-58, K. R. Road, Basavanagudi, Bengaluru 560 004
  E-mail: vivabangalore@vivagroupindia.net, Tel. 26607409, 26607410
- 101-102 Mughal Marc Apartments, 3-4-637 to 641, Narayanguda, Hyderabad 500 029
  E-mail: vivahyderabad@vivagroupindia.net, Tel. 27564481, 27564482
- Beevi Towers, First Floor, SRM Road, Kaloor, Kochi 682 018, Kerala
  E-mail: vivakochi@vivagroupindia.net, Tel: 0484-2403055, 2403056
- 232, GNB Road, Beside UCO Bank, Silpukhuri, Guwahati 781 003
  E-mail: vivaguwahati@vivagroupindia.net, Tel: 0361-2666386

www.vivagroupindia.com

Published by arrangement with
W. W. Norton & Company, Inc.
500 Fifth Avenue, New York
NY 10110

ISBN : 978-81-309-2662-9

Published by Vinod Vasishtha for Viva Books Private Limited, 4737/23, Ansari Road, New Delhi-110 002. Printed and bound in India.

For Robert and Rebecca,
August and Greta

Contents

Acknowledgments

David Hendin's brilliance and generous attention to two generations of Martins has made this and every other Miss Manners enterprise not only possible, but delightful.

The authors are also grateful to Angela von der Lippe and to Kimberley Heatherington.

Miss Manners®

MINDS YOUR BUSINESS

Introduction

How is your business any of Miss Manners' business?

Her own business model is founded on the hope of putting herself out of business. Perhaps your professional goal is different, but nothing would make her happier than to wake up one morning to a world in which her modest advice had been so absorbed that it required no further reinforcement. The porch swing beckons.

Alas. Her correspondence of late has convinced her that all you busy people out there are not solving your problems on your own—you are making them worse.

It's a wonder any work gets done, because, as the junior people explain, all the burden is on them, while their seniors are preoccupied with their pretentious social standing and their golf games. The senior staff complains of having to carry their juniors, who keep being distracted by their chaotic social arrangements, their awful music, and their violent video games.

Supervisors report that their employees don't practice the most basic manners, and that job applicants are worse. Workers report being treated with disrespect by their supervisors, and applicants report being ignored, not only when they apply, but even after being interviewed.

Customers report that clerks ignore or pressure them and clerks complain that customers yell and curse them. Employers report that employees are always goofing off during work hours and employees report that employers expect them to attend company functions in their free time.

If there is a professional dress code, some people are indignant because it inhibits their freedom of self-expression. If there is a casual dress standard, some people are indignant because of the free and uninhibited way others express themselves. If there is a speech code, some declare it is too weak to be of use and some that it stifles creativity or honesty or morale.

The old business luncheon is still an expected part of successful professional life, even though the martinis and the hat-check girls have long gone their separate—or possibly joint—ways. For those who have always gotten their sustenance straight from the refrigerator or the food court and have never actually sat down to a meal in company, having to go out and eat with a job interviewer, colleagues, or clients is a crisis.

If the younger generation can't eat, the older generation can't tweet. New fashions and new technologies continue to increase the list of required professional skills. Bosses who thought that sensitivity was for girls learned to navigate weekend retreats and touchy-feely seminars without being brought up on charges. When their secretaries were replaced by computers, the smarter ones accepted the unavoidable humiliation of being lectured to by a contemptuous teenager from the computer help desk. And then—having learned the hard way the results of pressing "send" on every angry email—they were asked to post blogs filled with chummy and pithy observations about the company that seemed spontaneous and intimate without sending the legal department into hysterics.

All these problems are symptomatic of wider cultural confusion that has left the workplace riddled with etiquette land mines. Whether you blame resistance to relaxing the old rigidity of behavior or ignorance of traditional businesslike behavior, everybody—not only between junior and senior groups, but within them as well—seems to be getting on everybody else's nerves.

Remember the good old days, when people just went about their business without all this irritation? No, you don't really. You weren't even there. Miss Manners, who was, assures you that the good old days had worse etiquette problems.

The rote courtesy that you imagine was then practiced was directed only toward self-designated gentlemen. Ladies, along with blacks, gays, and the disabled, were either excluded or exploited, a moral sin that led, as such things often do, to grievous manners sins.

When on the job, they, along with other underlings, were not accorded the respect they were supposed to show. For example, they were addressed by their first names, as if they were children, or called boys or girls by people whom they were expected to address using honorifics and surnames. If they objected to what we now call sexual harassment (then known as "fun") or bigotry, they were at best branded as having no sense of humor. More likely, they suffered the consequences of being identified as troublemakers.

Victims of that callousness are still around. Miss Manners wonders how they feel when total strangers address them in the old condescending way, under the pretense of friendliness.

At least the dress code was clear in the old days. Yes, and such items as jackets, ties, and nylon stockings were worn through scorching summers in non-air-conditioned offices. Those people looked professional right up until the moment they keeled over.

What you probably miss is the professional demeanor they were expected to maintain. Clerks did not make customers wait until they had finished their personal telephone calls. Waiters did not introduce themselves. Customer service representatives answered the telephone.

And if you are a clerk, a waiter, or a customer service representative, you long for the time when you would have been able to deal with people who give you their full attention and who keep their tempers under control.

When the deterioration of business manners finally became too serious a problem to ignore, the professional world took one look at the problem—and began shredding documents. While Miss Manners appreciates the fact that business has stopped ridiculing etiquette and admitted its legitimacy, this was not a courageous approach.

First to go was the purpose of good business manners. Miss Manners had thought that business manners existed to maintain personal dignity and to show respect for others while recognizing hierarchical privilege; to maintain a pleasant demeanor without invading others' privacy; to balance competitiveness with cooperation; to take responsibility but remain flexible; to be both attentive and discreet; and to combine honesty and tact. Instead, she was told that manners existed to dominate one's coworkers or to get rich, "good business manners" being edited, with a nearsighted eye on the bottom line, to be not manners at all but simply "good business."

And then the rules themselves went into the shredder, engulfed by almost universal agreement that there should be no difference between professional manners and personal manners. The relentless drive toward a less formal and less structured workplace resulted in the illusion that it was not work at all. If you did not have to wear a suit to the office, the reasoning went, it would not seem like work. If the boss throws a birthday party for you in the conference room, you will think of him not as your boss but as your friend.

At first, it was the women who suffered most from this confusion, and not only because they were expected to pick up the cake on the way to work. As women entered the higher echelons of the business world, no one told them that manners were context-dependent: On the contrary, a lady was supposed to be always a lady, or she would no longer be entitled to that once highly respectable designation. And she expected a gentleman always to be a gentleman.

But the gentlemen knew better. They shared that same set of manners for the social realm—the only place they encountered those ladies, because "office girls" didn't qualify. A gentleman would never brag, or discuss money or insist that he was right. (Miss Manners trusts that her Gentle Readers understand that she is referring to the rules in which they believed, not the way they actually behaved.) But they had another set of manners for the working world. Good business manners could hardly have forbidden them to talk about money, claim credit for their achievements, or fight for that which they believed to be right. Neither an officer-and-a-gentleman, nor a gentleman-and-a-scholar was expected to yield easily in his professional capacity. Meanwhile, their new female colleagues refrained from asking for raises, modestly demurred in connection with their achievements, and retreated when challenged.

You would think that the employer's motivation for blurring the distinction between the personal and the professional would have been transparent. If your coworkers are your family, then asking for a raise reverts to the childhood ritual of asking your parents to increase your allowance. Yet instead of the women learning from the men, the reverse happened.

And to Miss Manners' astonishment, at the very same time that terms like "paternalism" and "in loco parentis" were acquiring new and sinister meanings, the employees themselves have been enthusiastically embracing the fiction that "we're all one big family." They agonize over the choice of Secret Santa gifts for people they barely know, and are hurt when they are excluded from such once-family affairs as weddings and christenings.

This self-deception was not universal, but the confusion resulted in entirely new problems. Years ago, the company used to throw an annual Christmas party, at which the holiday cheer of some employees would be found to have exceeded the usual bounds. The most egregious cases would find themselves out on the street—or worse—while Miss Manners was sometimes able to help those whose behaviors had been merely mortifying.

At last it seemed that the cyclical downturns of the business cycle coupled with public indignation over corporate excess would solve that problem for all time. Christmas parties cost money and cut into profits, so businesspeople could solve the problem in a businesslike way by doing away with entertaining. Instead, the letters began to pour in from underpaid employees who were now being asked to bring the food (or at least pay for it) to a party they had not wanted to attend in the first place. And it's not just Christmas. Every day is someone's birthday or shower or retirement.

A similar evolution occurred in office furniture. The fight over which boss kept an "open door" policy and who got the corner office was swept away by the cubicle. This was promptly replaced by bickering over the abuse of newly public spaces. The noisy, not to mention smelly, eater, it turned out, could now be heard half a floor away—only partially drowned out by the employee who spent a good deal of his workday on the phone with his girlfriend.

At the same time, business manners came to be applied to personal life. It comes as no surprise to Miss Manners that people trained to think of such delightful things as profit and loss, cost and benefit, efficiency and whatever term we now use to deride the opposite, apply such concepts to their daily interactions. This does not work well.

It is now the common belief that the way to capture that whimsical and elusive thing called true love is to advertise, hold interviews, do background and financial checks, and insist on extensive internships, as it were, before the commitment of marriage. Afterward, as in the business world, there is no longer job security, and the equivalent of "You just don't seem to fit in" is justification for firing.

A business analysis of the ancient and sacred custom of hospitality reveals that the host pays all of the expenses. Instead of trusting that things will more or less even out through reciprocal hospitality, guests are settling their accounts on the spot. If hosts have not demanded advance payment, in the way of donated food or even cash, guests feel obliged to make an offering at the door.

Actual objects chosen by the donor are now given as presents at work, but friends and relatives are given bonuses when they achieve such goals as birthdays, graduations, weddings—and funerals, although the last are issued to their heirs. These may be in the form of cash, gift cards, or the purchase of items from lists supplied by the recipient. The element of thoughtfulness has been eliminated by mutual consent.

The worst is that while everyone agrees that family is of paramount importance, business is allowed to trump any personal obligation or occasion. A relaxed workplace has spread tension at home. Engagements, even serious ones to attend weddings and dinner parties, are skipped with this excuse, or guests use the time to receive and send messages that they justify as urgent business. And these are the same people who play video games and check their online auction bids at work.

The result is etiquette chaos. Miss Manners has to step in.

All right, times have changed. Miss Manners has been assured that the introduction of women into all levels of the workforce has rendered history obsolete. Or perhaps it was technology. Or the youthfulness of Internet tycoons. Or the cultural shift from suppressing ethnic identity to celebrating it. Or the greater oxygen flow that apparently results when a businessman sheds his necktie and a businesswoman her pantyhose.

Miss Manners emphatically does not advocate a return to old-style office behavior. Change was desperately needed, and, contrary to rumor, etiquette is not against change. It only stipulates that it be well thought out, orderly change that preserves what is good from the past while rectifying what is bad. In simple terms, this means ceding final authority to Miss Manners.

But change is now cited as an excuse for jettisoning the eternal virtues that underlie all civilized behavior and transcend societal development. Had she been consulted in advance, Miss Manners would never have permitted the oh-so-casual, we're-not-really-at-work atmosphere prevalent today. But she would also have scotched the always-tethered, work-trumps-all credo that tramples over personal commitments.

The abrasiveness of modern society, which Miss Manners recalls having mentioned once or twice before in the course of her career, has indeed infected the business world. But that is not the only problem. Well-meaning people find themselves in a new sort of etiquette trouble, both at work and in their personal lives, even as they struggle to do right in both of these realms.

The problem arises because they can no longer tell the difference between the two. Or which manners to use where.

It's time to make some changes.

Misplaced Social Manners

DEAR MISS MANNERS:

I am a lawyer at a large law firm in New York City. The hallway where my office is located is usually very quiet. However, in the past few months, a new secretary has taken a desk nearby. While she seems good-natured and competent, since she arrived I have been plagued by her near-constant chuckling.

I believe she is on the phone or online chatting with friends for much of the day, and while her conversations are very quiet, every five seconds or so a low, gurgling chuckle erupts from her desk. I don't need to work in total silence, but given the quietness of the hallway in general, this weird sound is driving me absolutely mad.

My firm generally has an open-door policy, but I find myself having to shut my door to get away from it. And I am not the only one; my neighbor has noticed the chuckling and is bothered by it as well.

How do I complain about this person's mirthful vocalizations without sounding like a crazy, happiness-hating person???

GENTLE READER:

Happiness? Isn't this supposed to be work?

Miss Manners sincerely hopes that you and the secretary are both happy with your jobs, and, indeed, that it is the object of your large law firm to restore happiness to your clients. Nevertheless, she cannot countenance your billing those clients extra for the work time you lost so that the secretary could socialize while on the job.

Of course you can shut your door. But for the sake of your colleagues, and perhaps of the secretary's career, she needs to be told (by her supervisor, if that is not your position) that her personal calls are disturbing others and should be made on her own time.

DEAR MISS MANNERS:

I'm not sure if this is a dilemma or an adjustment. I recently got hired in a wonderful position where I have freedom to create and have some major input as far as my job description goes. I don't usually make it a habit to sit and gossip with my coworkers.

Well, the other day the boss asked me to go into his office and he mentioned that the other coworkers commented about my isolating myself. I was honest with him and told him that I chose not to sit, have coffee, and gossip, as I had done this in previous positions and always regretted getting personal with previous coworkers, so that I consciously made the decision to just be professional.

I would like some advice on how to make everyone feel comfortable but not at my expense. I like my coworkers, and as far as I know I don't have any conflict with any of them, I just don't want to be more than coworkers. Is that right or wrong?

GENTLE READER:

My, the workplace has changed. Miss Manners remembers a time when pay scales may have been lower and working conditions may have been more rigid, but at least no working person had to fear being scolded by the boss for not spending enough time having coffee and gossiping with coworkers.

She couldn't agree with you more about avoiding the charade by which people pretend that they are not simply colleagues, but friends bound by personal ties. Friendships do sometimes develop among coworkers, but surely that should be a matter of individual choice, and be kept from interfering with the professionalism they should show on the job.

There is no use explaining that to your boss, who seems to lack the wit to understand your commitment to your job, or to your coffee-drinking, gossipy coworkers, who do not seem to share it. Your explanation, rather, should be that while you esteem your colleagues and feel privileged to work with them, you are just too excited about your work to take many breaks.

Misplaced Business Manners

DEAR MISS MANNERS:

Last year, I asked my husband's sister, who was having the family Thanksgiving dinner at her house, what I could bring. She insisted that it was easier for her to do it all herself and that we should just give her money.

I offered two more times to bring something, but she only wanted money. My husband did not agree and did not pay her when we ate at her house. When we arrived home, my husband's other sister called, screaming at him for not paying up.

This year, we would like to avoid being treated like deadbeat customers, but I'm not sure how we can best do so. Should we politely decline without a reason, should we go along with paying for our dinner for the sake of family harmony, or should we say we will come if we can participate as family members?

GENTLE READER:

It can't be easy to achieve harmony in a family in which screaming and charging for dinner pass for acceptable behavior.

Miss Manners doubts that your relatives are able to see the crucial difference between helping to cook for a family gathering and paying admission to attend it. In future, it would be good to give the dinner yourself, setting an example of hospitality.

This year, she suggests that you offer to do the grocery shopping, asking your sister-in-law for a list, and refusing even partial payment on the grounds that you wouldn't feel right charging family or friends. Think of it as an investment.

Part 1

The Basics

CHAPTER 1

Getting In

"Just be yourself," your parents told you. "You'll be fine, just as you are."

Even as advice for a first romance, it was not to be taken literally. They did not mean you to show up in your favorite smelly sweat clothes and post your emotions on your social network. The hope was that you would calm down enough to seem relaxed, witty, intriguing, and hard-to-get. Or at least the oddly efficacious teenage substitutes—sullen, sarcastic, odd, and bored.

When applied to the professional world, this is bad advice from good people. Employees who are just being themselves are busy texting their friends when you are waiting for them to tell you where your size is or to realize what a brilliant presentation you are making at the meeting. They are chomping, snorting, wheezing, overflowing their cubicles, and neglecting to wash the coffee pot. They are supplying evidence for being denied promotions or being fired.

When attempting to enter the business world, you need to learn to be someone else. It is called having a professional identity. The job interviewer is seeking an employee who will lighten her own load, not make the workday more exciting. And as she already has a job, it is your mission to impress her, not the other way around.

Think of a job interview as a theatrical audition, although not for *A Chorus Line,* the eternal musical in which hopeful dancers find that baring their souls is more important than what they do at the barre.

- A good auditionee—like a good job candidate—is excited, energetic, and above all interested in the work to be done. Please spare Miss Manners your protest that demonstrating an interest that you do not feel is dishonest—that this wasn't your first choice and isn't your career goal. There you go, being yourself again. You are interested in obtaining the job, aren't you? The boss may be in the midst of a midlife crisis, cursing the day he took up the noble profession of waste management. That does not mean he is looking for someone as burned-out as he is.
- A good auditionee knows his lines. To show up at a job interview unaware of the industry's prospects or the company's mandate is, and will appear, lazy. If you are unwilling to extend such minimal effort in return for a promise of future salary and benefits, it is not hard to predict that you are even less likely to do so once the reality has cleared your checking account. And do not expect a warm reception for assurances that you can learn something you are already supposed to know. If the job description requires particular skills, the interview is a bit late to consider acquiring them.
- A good auditionee looks and sounds the part. The days of typing tests are mostly gone; it is the unusual job for which an applicant can objectively demonstrate his ability. As most bosses have learned, a degree is a poor proxy for competence, and a career spent doing the job for which one is applying raises as many questions as it answers. In these days of lawsuits and human resources departments, personal references can be hard to come by and harder to trust.

As a result, looking the part has increased in importance. Of all the areas in which you should not express your real self, dressing like You instead of like Them ranks right up there with putting your feet on the interviewer's desk, bumming a cigarette, and discussing your love life.

Think of the whole experience as an exercise in that most entrepreneurial and American of all pastimes: reinventing oneself. Your parents love you for what you are, so they learn to tolerate what you do. An employer will learn to tolerate what you are if he can love you for what you do.

THE APPROACH

DEAR MISS MANNERS:

Oh, I am at the breaking point.

I work for a temporary agency, where my main responsibility is finding people jobs. Each time I answer the telephone, I am amazed at what I hear coming from the other end.

I fear I am losing my patience with people who start their conversations:

"How you doin' today?"

"Did someone beep me?"

"You got any jobs available?"

"Did someone there call me?"

Many times, these people sound like they have just awakened, or there's a TV blaring in the background.

It has been my experience that it's much easier to answer any questions if the caller first identifies him or herself. Many times they try, but all I get is "This is Bill"—and I meet many Bills each week.

I believe that anyone in search of a job should be willing to make telephone work as easy as possible on the potential employer by identifying who they are and why they are calling. I do not appreciate people asking me how I'm doing when it may be none of their business.

GENTLE READER:

It is certainly not a good idea for job applicants to annoy the person in charge of finding them jobs. You get no argument from Miss Manners there. But there is a reason greater than your pique for disqualifying these callers from jobs, if you would like to use this to justify your personal reaction. And that is that the applicants have just demonstrated that they are ignorant of professional manners.

Closet Anxiety

DEAR MISS MANNERS:

I am a college student, about to graduate and get out in the workforce. I have heard and seen that most people choose to dress conservatively at an interview. How conservative should I go? Am I allowed to wear a pantsuit or is the skirt suit the only choice for me?

I don't like conservatism in general and I like to be able to show a touch of my personality and style in the way I dress.

What would you mostly recommend for college females ready to get out in the real world? Is this the time when dressing conservative is the ultimate best choice?

GENTLE READER:

Miss Manners hopes it doesn't disappoint you to hear that pantsuits are no longer considered cutting-edge. Female senators wear them to work.

The rule about interviews is to dress for the job you want. Perhaps there are fields in which college students are sought for their personalities and style, in which case you would do well to exhibit yours. For prospective employers who hire people for their skills or industry, this might be a sign that you are more interested in displaying yourself than in fitting in.

THE INTERVIEW

"Notice that she didn't say anything about her family," complained a member of the search committee. "I wouldn't trust someone who can't talk about her feelings—or who's not willing to be open with us."

He preferred the candidate who told the committee how he had dealt with his wife's leaving him (illustrating his progress from destructive anger to acceptance to finding someone wonderful), his son's learning disability, and his daughter's depression.

The decision was between that candidate and the one who said she used to go to pieces when men treated her badly but has learned to love herself and is now closer to her children. As it was put by one of the people in charge of finding the best person for the job—which had to do with handling money rather than emotions—"You can just tell from the way she talked about it that she's an honest, caring person."

Maybe yes, maybe no, muses cynical Miss Manners.

Miss Manners would not dream of suggesting that job seekers might tailor their histories to fit what potential employers want to hear. But word certainly has gotten around that in the upper reaches of the job market, the successful candidate tells personal stories, preferably featuring a confession of some frailty now conquered.

Why this works, Miss Manners is not exactly sure. A fair-minded employer would overlook problems, especially past problems, in favor of compensating strengths. The puzzling part is how these came to be considered positive assets.

It was odd enough, Miss Manners thought, when the willingness to confide in strangers (other than those in the healing professions) was taken to be a sign of recovering emotional health. It was odder still when it became a sign of character—and reluctance to do so an indication of wiliness, if not deceit.

If you want to hire someone to paint your house, you will probably not be reassured by a candidate's bringing up a drinking problem, no matter how far in the past. When interviewing babysitters, you are not likely to be encouraged by being made privy to a candidate's bad luck with romance.

So why would anyone actively seek an employee who brings private concerns into a job interview? Either these are irrelevant to the job, in which case there is no point in bringing them up, or they are relevant, in which case a prospective employer, however sympathetic, would have to ask how they might impinge on the job.

The response that has been made to Miss Manners is roughly as follows:

1. Personnel problems are an inevitable part of any high-ranking job, and nowadays it's hard to know where the latest emotional land mines might be. We have people who were behaving well by yesterday's standards who have failed to recognize danger signals and gotten us into serious trouble. So the safest person is one who is sensitive—who understands where all this is coming from. A history of problems shows familiarity with them. Someone who has been hurt and worked it through is less likely to hurt others or to be oblivious to their feelings.
2. You can't check everything about a person, and many organizations have been taken in by smooth types who have lied about themselves. If we uncover something bad we haven't heard about, we assume that we've been deliberately misled. But if we hear it from the candidate, it's different. We take that as evidence of willingness to come clean. When the person confesses the worst, you don't worry so much about being hit with unpleasant surprises.
3. Personal problems—addictions, family disputes, and such—may not be more common than they used to be, but people are more

> likely to allow them to intrude on job performance. If you know what they are up-front, you can choose the ones you are willing to deal with.

In the face of these arguments, Miss Manners' preference for privacy seems like a fastidious old prejudice. Even the British royal family has abandoned the concept of the stiff upper lip in favor of the quivering lip. So rather than blabber about dignity, she will confine herself to the issue of how such personal talk should be interpreted when weighing candidates for jobs.

If the job is one where loyalty to the company and discretion about its plans are important, is it wise to hire someone who freely discusses family matters and sensitive matters that involve other people? What happens when someone who believes in telling all is trusted with the problems of employees who may want them kept confidential?

If private lives are part of the employment record, people feel forced to discuss them, although the ratio of candor to canniness in presenting job qualifications is probably no differently applied than to explanations of why these candidates are leaving their present jobs.

But doesn't this go against everything we have learned since the bad old days when single women were asked if they planned to get married (on the assumption that they would then quit), married women were asked if they planned to have children (on the assumption that they would then quit), mothers were asked how they cared for their children (on the assumption that they would neglect the job), and older women weren't asked anything because it was just assumed they were cranky and bitter?

Nowadays, such questions are illegal. As it is probably not a good idea to threaten to sue a potential employer, the only answer should be, "I can assure you that my personal life will not interfere with my doing the job." If we knew that mistakes immunized people against making further mistakes, it might be reasonable to trust the person with the blemished record. But since we don't, it doesn't seem fair to penalize the clean record.

And finally, do we really want to work that hard to discourage professionalism?

Questionable Questions

DEAR MISS MANNERS:

We, the jobless minority, expect to be rejected most of the time. And we do not blame companies for this. However, I have observed a proliferation of ungracious behavior from people with whom I have come in contact during my career quest.

Few people realize that even though they may not be in a position to hire anyone, they can offer much valuable information to job seekers. Information such as contact names, the names of companies that they have heard are hiring, critical advice on tactics, or detailed information about inroads into a company are sincerely appreciated.

I have faced an onslaught of probing personal questions, such as "What is the most difficult thing you have ever done in your life?" Is the true answer to this question work-related for anyone?

I have been asked questions that seem to beg insincere replies, such as "What is your worst fault?" (I have been advised to respond with a fault that is really a positive characteristic—"I am too much of a perfectionist.")

This strikes me as dishonest, and I don't like to engage in competitions in which the dishonest prevail. Interviews are for assessing qualifications and professionalism, not psychology. To discover a person's true character, try his or her references.

I know that as a job seeker, my etiquette must be superb. I must be on time; I must send prompt thank-you notes; I must burn no bridges. However, I would ask everyone who is faced with the annoyance of inquiries from job seekers to have compassion and consider that today's job seeker may be tomorrow's client, or, even worse, tomorrow's boss.

GENTLE READER:

How much worse does unemployment have to get before those with power over job seekers realize that it is not a good idea to misuse their power to be rude because they could easily soon be on the receiving end?

This probably sounds as if Miss Manners wrecked the economy for the purpose of getting people into the proper frame of mind for learning and appreciating etiquette. She does go to great lengths to make this point, but not that far.

Certainly, she agrees that politeness is as essential on the part of the person doing the interviewing as on the part of the person who, being anxious about getting the job, may see a more immediate need to appear to advantage.

She also agrees that suggestions about openings elsewhere are extra-polite (not required, but deserving of special credit), and that silly personal questions are outrageous, although this is more likely to come from the rude idea that this relates to job performance than from vulgar curiosity.

The unemployed are badly enough off without being subjected to a barrage of rude personal comments. But your idea of being given a critique, along with a refusal, is fraught with danger. These people have already failed to distinguish between the personal and the professional. What makes you think they will be able to do so when invited to offer criticism?

DEAR MISS MANNERS:

During a job interview where I met with the Vice President of Human Resources, it was obvious that she had a raspy voice and a cough. I assumed that she had a cold or other minor/temporary condition and waited for a cue ("Please excuse my voice; I have a cold") to offer sympathy or concern.

When none came, I did not make any comment at all, assuming that she did not want to call attention (!) to her situation. The interview ended 45 minutes later with absolutely no mention of her condition. Should I have made a comment ("Gee, that's a nasty cough") without waiting for a direct opening? Or did I behave appropriately?

GENTLE READER:

Miss Manners is pleased to reassure you that you did not fail the job interview by demonstrating, in one well-meant statement, that you lacked both discretion and experience.

To initiate a personal comment, even a sympathetic one, to a job interviewer is intrusive. To assume that you can correctly diagnose a stranger as having a temporary cold, when her voice could simply be raspy or she could have a serious disease, is naïve. Neither is a quality one looks for in an employee.

Legitimate Questions

DEAR MISS MANNERS:

If an applicant is asked about his salary requirements, what is the proper way to answer? Is it polite to question why a previous employee left or was fired? If a company representative says he'll call, should one be persistent if he doesn't? Is it polite to inquire as to why one wasn't hired and someone else was?

GENTLE READER:

Miss Manners can hardly think of a job in which polite persistence—the determination to pursue one's objective without actually becoming a pest—is not a virtue. If handled properly, this should suggest that the employer need only employ you to get you to stop going after him or her and start going after the company's interests.

This includes showing enthusiastic interest in the company, asking intelligent questions, proposing a salary for oneself that is in the high range of reasonableness, writing afterward to thank the employer for the interview, and calling to find out whether a decision has been made.

It does not, however, involve asking indiscreet questions about one's predecessor or one's successful rival. In case the company should have another opening, you don't want the employer to have had to come up with an argument as to why you wouldn't do.

DEAR MISS MANNERS:

I often find myself in an awkward position of having to address issues related to the fact that I don't have a college degree. I don't want to make excuses, because I value education. Suffice it to say that I accept responsibility for my choices.

As a professional woman in a high-profile job who worked hard to achieve success, I enjoy a good reputation amongst my peers and my superiors. Many people in my organization have come to rely on my expertise in the areas of analysis and liaison.

Because of the position I hold, I'm frequently asked what my background is, where I went to school, and what degree I possess. I always answer truthfully, and the response is usually one of shock or discomfort, followed by a remark such as, "I'd never have been able to tell." Also, I'm often a witness to conversations in which executive managers disparage those who don't have degrees and set hiring policies that make possession of a degree a prerequisite for particular jobs. Interestingly, they don't care whether the degree has any correlation to the job.

GENTLE READER:

It makes perfect sense to Miss Manners. They know your work; therefore, how you acquired your knowledge and skills is so unimportant to them that they probably don't remember, when they mention the need for degrees, that you don't have one.

When it comes to hiring, however, they are dealing with strangers and are looking for clues that candidates are prepared to do the job. We all know that a degree is no guarantee of competence, but it is supposed to certify a basic standard, so it serves as a starting point.

That people are amazed that you educated yourself should be a source of pride to you, and you can acknowledge it truthfully without devaluing education by saying, "I did it the hard way, although I can't say I would recommend this to others." Others who nevertheless did so would benefit from your reminding your colleagues to be on the lookout for extraordinary people who, like yourself, were motivated to learn without the benefit of tests and deadlines.

The Extended Interview

DEAR MISS MANNERS:

A candidate our department was interviewing spent 30 minutes with each member of the existing staff during the day, and later we went as a group with our spouses to dinner. During my half hour, we discussed matters pertaining to the university job, since I thought that general topics, such as the quality of the local schools, would be more appropriate at dinner when spouses could also contribute.

The food at dinner was fine, but at the point where people had stopped chewing and a table-wide conversation could ensue, the wife of the department head, who had several drinks under the sash, began a long monologue concerning details of her garden, her trips to Europe, her children, his children, and their children. The interview candidate shrank into insignificance, while the department head sat there with a grin on his face. No one else spoke until we broke up to leave.

The candidate declined the job offer. Is there some way I could have set the conversation back on a course that would focus on the reason 15 people were invited for dinner? I have tenure and thought later that this might have been an occasion to use it pointedly, but can't think of a good way.

GENTLE READER:

The last Miss Manners heard, the academic job market was not so good that candidates could afford to turn down jobs for no more pressing reason than that the department head's wife got tight and boring at dinner.

However, the question of what is expected of spouses is a not inconsiderable factor in weighing a job offer. As you undoubtedly know from interviewing candidates, many have spouses who will require their own new jobs if they are to move. In any case, the candidate's spouse will want to know what she would be taking on if he accepts the job.

Suppose he reports, "All the spouses showed up at dinner, so I imagine you'd be expected to, too"? That alone might have put her off, and the additional information that the dinner was dominated by a bore would not have helped.

One helpful thing you might do is to make it clear to candidates that such a dinner is prompted by staff and spouses' friendly interest and hope of being useful in answering questions he might have about the area—making the point that a spouse could be as much or little involved in after-hours department functions as she liked.

This also sets up the immediate squelch you requested for the chairman's wife. The proper one is not "Pipe down, honey, and your husband can't defend you because I have tenure" but "Why don't we first entice him here by telling him about what a charming place this is to live—then, if he joins the department, we can think about making friends."

THE FOLLOW-UP

DEAR MISS MANNERS:

I am searching for a new job, and have written several thank-yous to those who have interviewed me. My usual thank-you notes are handwritten on neutral (not cutesy) informal fold-over cards. My sister was horrified at this, and insisted the proper form is a formal business letter, printed on the same type of paper one would use for a résumé. Which is more appropriate?

GENTLE READER:

Each of you has focused on a different—and, as you have noticed, contradictory—purpose behind interview thank-you letters. Your sister wants to emphasize how businesslike you are, and by extension, how fit for the job. You are trying to separate yourself from the other applicants by making your letter more personal. Both are possible: there is nothing wrong with a handwritten note on formal stationery. In truth, you have probably already singled yourself out by sending any note at all.

Anybody There?

DEAR MISS MANNERS:

I am a recent college grad and have been applying for jobs online. Most of these jobs require that applicants send a résumé to an email address, and there is no number to call or an address (to apply in person).

I have received very few responses or even replies that they received my résumé, which is the problem. I don't know if it wound up in a spam folder or was deleted. If that is the case, I would like to send it again. But if they received it and just didn't want to hire me, I wouldn't want to send it again and seem like a pest.

If you apply for a job online, shouldn't they at least let you know they received your résumé, even if they don't hire you, so at least you would know it didn't disappear in cyberworld?

GENTLE READER:

Yes, they should. But nowadays, businesses plead understaffing—compounded by the great number of people looking for work—to excuse the lack of feedback they give to job applicants. As if they had never heard of using form replies, which is easier than ever with email—and as if they hadn't been just as unresponsive when times were flush.

Beleaguered as they are, they are not likely to be noticeably worse off if you resend your message, mentioning that you had not heard back. Miss Manners has heard that some employers consider eagerness to be a virtue.

The Brush-Off

DEAR MISS MANNERS:

I have been conducting a job search for over a year now, applying for positions at many different universities, and have received numerous rejection letters.

I have noticed a pattern developing. With very few exceptions, the most prestigious universities in the nation have been responsible for some of the least gracious correspondence I have ever experienced. Some letters have been downright insulting!

Meanwhile, I have received letters that left me feeling favorably impressed, from institutions that are anything but elitist. I was raised to believe that sensitivity to the feelings of others is, in itself, a mark of personal distinction. How can so many highly regarded academic institutions employ so many ill-bred people and not have their reputations suffer?

GENTLE READER:

Because those are their recent graduates who can't get jobs elsewhere. Also, because although any institution that is more sought-after than seeking may know that its reputation will suffer, many also believe that behaving insufferably is a sign of distinction. Miss Manners wishes to point out two serious mistakes in this rude way of thinking.

The first is that arrogant people are much more likely to be perceived as uneducated louts than as important people who can't be bothered to be polite. Thus, the victims of this rudeness, far from believing themselves to have been scorned by their betters, are bound to have (and to spread) doubts about the quality of an institution that has such low-grade employees.

The second is that every institution makes personnel mistakes, but to insult, as well as merely to reject, people who might turn out to be raging successes later can be devastating. The more powerful these people turn out to be, the more they will enjoy telling how they were misjudged and mistreated. No institution should risk setting itself up as the butt of such a story.

Questionable Applications

DEAR MISS MANNERS:

As the managing partner of a law firm, I receive a steady stream of (mostly) unsolicited letters from attorneys seeking a position at the firm. I say "mostly," because occasionally we advertise for an attorney with specific qualifications, e.g., expertise in water law.

Yet, even when the advertisement is very specific, I receive dozens of letters and résumés from attorneys who do not meet the specified qualifications. Clearly, these people are simply taking a shot in the dark and hoping for the best. Do good manners and etiquette require me to respond to all these letters?

GENTLE READER:

Funny that you should ask about the obligations of both manners and etiquette. Miss Manners makes a distinction between them, with manners being the principles of courteous behavior and etiquette being the rules that apply to a particular situation.

No, etiquette does not require that you reply to unsolicited job applications. However, it does require a response to candidates you have interviewed, a courtesy often neglected.

But Miss Manners begs you to consider the state of mind of the job seeker: hope, followed by increasingly painful doubt. Finally, the silence indicates that the application, complete with this person's professional history and hopes, was regarded as trash. Could you not find a minute to say, "Sorry, we're looking for an expert in water law"? Even people who don't follow instructions have feelings.

DEAR MISS MANNERS:

I am interested in the etiquette of informing applicants of errors in their résumés.

As the primary contact for staffing in our company, I recently received a résumé from an applicant which used the word "tenet" instead of "tenant" in several instances. I dismissed the applicant completely because I believe if there is one thing you should proofread, it would be your résumé! Having been in this field for many years, I know that most of my colleagues feel the same way—they won't even consider a résumé with typographical, spelling, punctuation, and grammatical errors.

What I am torn about is whether or not to inform this applicant that they are sending out a document that is damaging their chances of obtaining employment. Is it rude to point out the flaws in a case like this one?

GENTLE READER:

Correcting other people's writing is rude, unless you are authorized to do so. This is why Miss Manners will say nothing to you about pairing single subjects with plural pronouns.

However, it is a common complaint of job seekers that they are left wondering why they were rejected. It would be within your purview to let them know, in a matter-of-fact way, that you are sorry to inform them that they will not be hired because you and your colleagues disqualify those who have sent résumés that contain mistakes in the use of language.

Pay-Offs

DEAR MISS MANNERS:

I have always viewed being asked to write a letter of recommendation as an honor. Even the slightest hesitation or question about what to write causes me to express my appreciation at being asked but my respectful decline.

During the last few months, I have provided some 20 such prompt and thoughtful letters of reference, several on behalf of two individuals, with copies sent to them as a courtesy. The positions being sought are at the senior executive level. In a number of cases, the employer has called to indicate what a particularly outstanding letter I sent.

Is it reasonable to expect some expression of thank-you in return? A letter of recommendation or reference is given freely and willingly, so is it correct to expect a thank-you?

It feels like it to me. Although I recall being taught that a gift given with the expectation of something in return was never a gift at all, I was brought up to say thank you and to write notes. I wonder if a part of the decline in business behavior and standards is related to what feels like a loss of very fundamental social grace.

GENTLE READER:

Please stop repeating that rude old saw about the meanness of expecting to be thanked. Miss Manners assures you that that idea has made no small contribution to the very problem of which you complain.

Being thanked is a perfectly reasonable expectation after trying to please someone. It is, in fact, the acknowledgment that one's efforts have actually succeeded.

Without cunningly plotting to put someone else in one's debt through feigned generosity—which is what you make it sound like—a kind person could imagine that a lack of demonstrated appreciation springs from a true lack of appreciation. That is why Miss Manners advises those whose presents are greeted with silence to stop giving what is apparently not wanted.

She would not go so far as to claim that every letter of recommendation requires its own letter of thanks. Evaluating employees for future employment is a routine task of business. But when special effort is made, as seems to be the case with you, it should be acknowledged. You would be justified in taking at their word those who believe that writing letters is passé, interpreting it to include letters of recommendation.

DEAR MISS MANNERS:

As a result of referring an acquaintance for employment at the company for which I work, I will be receiving a generous referral bonus.

I was informed by this person that I should thank him appropriately—hinting strongly that I should share the money with him. I was taken by surprise, especially since I felt that he should have at least thanked me first for influencing his hiring. I am not sure that I feel like sharing now.

What is the etiquette in this situation? Is there a percentage of my referral award that I am expected to share, even if the person being hired is getting a generous raise, a better position, and a good benefits package? What is the least awkward way of presenting the person with a share of the money?

GENTLE READER:

Miss Manners assures you that one thing you don't have to worry about with extortionists is being smooth and subtle about how you meet their demands. The chances of this person's being offended if you threw money at him strike her as being slight.

But she fails to see why you would do this. Miss Manners would be more inclined to remember that her employer rewarded her for giving personnel advice. Perhaps the loyal thing to do would be to confess that unfortunately you have led him to hire someone who expects kickbacks.

Avoiding the Consequences

DEAR MISS MANNERS:

I recently took a new job offer and had planned to start in six weeks. Since I accepted, my future employer reported disastrous second-quarter earnings and made a bunch of layoffs. They assured me during the interview that the company was rock-solid. Obviously this is not the case and I've decided not to take the job after all. But I don't want to burn bridges. What's a professional and tactful way to break the news to the guy who hired me?

GENTLE READER:

Without questioning the practical basis of your decision, Miss Manners feels obligated to point out that it is not easy to demonstrate what a principled employee you are while in the very act of breaking your word.

She begs you not to give in to the temptation to go on the offensive and point out that his word about the state of the company was not trustworthy, either. There is a somewhat tactful way to phrase this—"I didn't fully understand the situation"—but it definitely burns bridges.

Your best hope is to cast this vaguely as a matter of conflicting ethics—"I never should have accepted this, because I have obligations that make it wrong for me to make the switch"—accompanied by profuse apologies. The fact that the obligation is to your career, rather than to your present employer or your anxious family, need not be made clear.

DEAR MISS MANNERS:

Last year I quit a job I'd held for six years to join a dotcom. My new employer just filed Chapter 11, and I'd like to return to my former employer. I enjoyed this job, received good performance reviews, and left on good terms. I only left because the dotcom offered me a leadership position that wasn't available in my company. How can I approach my old boss?

GENTLE READER:

Not with your tail between your legs. Miss Manners wanted to state this in positive terms, not negative, but when she attempted to describe how the tail should be held, it began to sound obscene.

What she is trying to say is that you should approach your old boss jauntily, not guiltily. Tell him that although you regret the fate of the dotcom because of the other people connected with it, you can't help feeling relieved on your own behalf, because you loved your job with him, and you missed it.

True, he can still say, "You should have thought of that before you left." But he will at least have to say this in good spirits and keep you pleasantly in mind. There is a major manners lesson here. You may have quit in good form because you genuinely liked your old job, but it is the wise as well as the polite thing to do in any case.

Rewarding Internship

DEAR MISS MANNERS:

My daughter is a college intern at a doctor's office, working as a Web designer. The doctor is presenting a documentary and afterward they will have a banquet. The Admin Manager, her direct supervisor, asked my daughter if she would attend the banquet to serve wine to the guests. My daughter was insulted. For one thing it would be on her own time for free labor. Secondly, she feels like she shouldn't have to serve the people she works with. As an intern, should she be insulted?

GENTLE READER:

From your first objection, Miss Manners gathers that this is a paid internship—at least for time spent in the office. She would therefore advise your daughter to forgo being insulted and instead settle for finding that—like many employees asked to work overtime without compensation—she unfortunately has an unavoidable prior commitment.

Even unpaid interns, who are too often treated as if that reflected their worth, should refrain from nursing grudges. All interns are right to expect to be compensated in experience and gratitude, but they should remember that an internship is an extended audition, and exercise enthusiasm, competence—and restraint.

CHAPTER 2

Getting Out

If the boss brags that his company is like a family, check the unemployment lines. You are likely to find his grandmother, whom he holds dear and values for her past service, but who was just not producing as she used to. His definition of loyalty is apt to be yours for himself, and he knows how to shame ingrates who want their allowances raised.

When families are split, at least each side is usually left with sympathizing relatives and friends. The office family offers no such support. It's not just the fired slacker who complains of being deserted after years of shared lunches and gossip; it's also the beloved retiree whom everyone hates to see go. Tragically, it is at this vulnerable time that most people finally understand the importance of making real friends outside of work. Those whose friendship is prorated with your last paycheck are known as coworkers.

Job terminations, whether they are voluntary or involuntary, at the beginning of a career or at the end, are bound to be painful for everyone.

And that includes the underpaid, overworked winner of the lottery who is newly experiencing the envy and greed of others.

The fired employee is worrying about finding employment; the quitter has the uncertainty of what the new job will be like; the retiree wonders what he will do with his time. Coworkers fear for their own jobs and increased workloads. The boss frets over hiring and training a replacement, getting the work done, maintaining customer relations and keeping up office morale—plus the possible reappearance of what is described in the news as "a disgruntled former employee."

What helps in emotional situations is formality and ceremony, not, as popularly believed, talking things out, which can easily lead to disaster. Companies used to recognize this with retirement parties, speeches, and gold watches. It lifted morale, not by pretending to be family, but by being seen as appreciative of long-term professional effort. Slashed budgets have left this to be improvised by colleagues or actual relatives, which is better than nothing, but not the same.

Even in cases of involuntary terminations or redundancies or downsizings or layoffs or sackings—or whatever the euphemism for being thrown out on the street—some dignity is possible. The cause, now that it has gone this far, should be immaterial to the behavior. Everyone, and that includes the employee caught stealing and reselling the toner, should be treated with formal politeness. The thief may need to be watched a bit more closely on the way out the door, but it is important to distinguish between reasonable precaution and unnecessary humiliation.

Most important is what is not said on both sides. Firers and colleagues should resist the temptation to offer comfort by telling the fired employee that he or she probably did not want to stay anyway. This gives as much solace as telling the bereaved that their relative is better off dead. And the person who is fired must resist telling everyone what they can do with the job.

LAYOFFS, DOWNSIZING, AND BEING FIRED

DEAR MISS MANNERS:

Help! I need to lay off 50 members of my staff. I'm a young manager and have never fired anyone before. Some of these employees are much older than me and have families to support. Can you give me a primer on how to fire someone?

GENTLE READER:

You are not too young to have broken off a romance, Miss Manners supposes, nor to have been on the receiving end of such a break.

She is far from suggesting that you should therefore know how to sever a connection painlessly. If you were so heartless as to find those experiences painless, you would not be interested in acquiring more finesse than it takes to say "Yeah, yeah—skip the sob story, just take your stuff and be out of here by five."

What she expects you to have learned, and to be able to transfer to this situation, is that there is no such thing as a painless dismissal. Nobody likes being fired, not even those who were planning to quit anyway. The kindest method is therefore not to worry about justifying your action more than is legally necessary, but to allow the other person to retain some dignity.

Paradoxically, this means making the firing impersonal, although gently so. Ending a person's job, like ending a romance, is not the time for recriminations; that turns the target either antagonistic or falsely optimistic. Rather you should blame circumstances (vague references to "the climate" or "restructuring" being the professional equivalent of vague declarations of needing to find oneself), set out the best terms within your power, and accept as inevitable that you will be resented.

DEAR MISS MANNERS:

I am in a quandary. A guy I hired earlier this year isn't working out. He's nice enough, but he hasn't been able to complete any projects on time and makes frequent errors. Invariably I have to ask a staffer to step in and help him out, which is a drain on resources that I can't afford. Under normal circumstances, I would simply let him go. However, I found out through the grapevine that he is going through a difficult divorce. Is it morally reprehensible to fire him? Should I give him some slack and let him keep his job for now even though he's not cutting the mustard?

GENTLE READER:

How much slack were you thinking of giving?

Miss Manners believes that a humane workplace must keep a supply of slack that it can use when deserving employees need it. Sick leave has been institutionalized to recognize the fact that even the most valued and hardworking people get sick, but they also have other life problems. Presumably, you excuse people to attend their grandmothers' funerals, provided they don't have an unreasonable number of grandmothers.

Here, however, you are dealing with an employee who has yet to prove his worth. It is surely time for a performance review. You cannot bring up the question of his divorce, but if he uses it to plead for some of that slack, you can certainly decide whether to give him any and if so, how much.

You do not owe him a living because he is unhappy, so it depends on whether you want to take a chance on him. However, if you don't set a time limit for the next performance review, you could find yourself carrying him through readjustment to the dating scene, and the ups and downs of subsequent romances.

It's Not That They Fired Me, It's How They Did It

DEAR MISS MANNERS:

I used to feel that having an answering machine was a courtesy, but now I'm not so sure.

The company I had worked for, over three years, lost its lease. I was having a continuing long-distance dialogue with the owner about my employment, attending to customers from my home while he searched for a new location. This required many phone calls to headquarters, each call an opportunity to talk to me in person.

One day I emerged from the shower to play back a message in which he informed me I was "let go" and should start job-hunting. This seemed to be his way of avoiding saying goodbye in a more personal way. I was very hurt.

GENTLE READER:

Your boss is a coward, Miss Manners is sorry to tell you. Or perhaps not so sorry, as he is now your former boss.

This does not excuse him from the need to be polite. The polite coward who cannot manage to deliver this unpleasant news face to face is still obliged to do so with the formality such a solemn action demands. He could have written you a letter.

Handling the Embarrassment

DEAR MISS MANNERS:

I am currently unemployed, single, with no children. I would like to be employed again. What do I say to people when they ask, "What do you do?"

In this society, it is what you do that matters, and not much else. When appropriate, I tell people I'm unemployed and I will also ask them if they know of any jobs. However, there are times when I feel it is inappropriate to answer the question with "I'm unemployed." Some people subsequently treat me like pond scum once they find out I'm unemployed. (You'd be surprised how often this happens.) I would like an appropriate response to "What do you do?"

GENTLE READER:

Even when this question is posed as an innocuous conversation-opener, and not by one of those dreadful people who uses social occasions to angle for professional advantage, Miss Manners finds it tedious. She was about to sympathize with you and advise you to treat it as if it were the more general question, "Tell me about yourself."

But hold on. You want to use social occasions to angle for a professional advantage. If you want to hear about job opportunities, you are going to have to tell people what kinds of jobs you can do. The upbeat way of saying "I'm unemployed and desperate" is "As a matter of fact, I'm just now looking for something challenging."

DEAR MISS MANNERS:

My husband is leaving—that is, he's been railroaded out of—a prominent job as a public servant in a small town. He has been very badly treated and we are angry and hurt, but are trying to hold onto our dignity. I want to give everyone within earshot a piece of my mind, but I know it won't do any good; their minds are closed.

What can I say when people ask why we are moving on? I want to take the high road and give them as little material as possible for the gossip mill. There is no other job in sight at this point, so we can't say that; he is just beginning a search. We need agreeable-sounding phrases that are not lies, and I'm stumped.

GENTLE READER:

Not "He's planning to spend more time with his family." They're on to that one, to the extent that it will start rumors of divorce. They are also on to "doing consulting," at least in Washington, where that means "out of office." And "looking at his options" is unkindly interpreted to mean that he doesn't have any worth talking about.

In your case, Miss Manners would actually advise saying, "He's out of office right now." Not that she thinks you owe anyone such bald truth. Her reasoning is: first, that as it is a small town, everyone knows the situation, so any euphemism will sound defensive; second, that it may remind those who feel he was treated unfairly to help.

However, Miss Manners understands that what you are really after is a safe form of revenge. All right, it is "Well, he's thinking of writing a book."

Now don't tell her that this is a lie. Everyone who feels badly treated is thinking of writing a book about it. And it never fails to get the rattled attention of those who mistreated the aspiring author.

DEAR MISS MANNERS:

I just quit a horrible job with a very well-known movie studio after one year of suffering. Most people "ooh and aah" when they hear where I was working. What's the best way to let them know that I no longer work there? I've tried to say "I resigned and am no longer with the company," but everyone seems to pry endlessly as to why anyone would want to leave such a place—of course, not knowing that the place was more like a concentration camp than anything remotely resembling a pleasant work environment. What's the best way to let them know that their probing questions are none of their business?

GENTLE READER:

Here's your line: "It was a matter of my artistic integrity. I'm afraid I can't really explain it any better than that." Please try to say it apologetically so it doesn't sound arrogant.

Miss Manners is aware that the assumption will be that you wanted to work on films about the homeless and the studio wanted to make films about blowing up the world. She also knows that this will excite the curious even more, and they will continue to besiege you. But it will shift the subject from employment to aesthetics and thus, she promises you, quickly exhaust people who had hoped to hear inside stories about movie stars.

The Boss Wasn't the Problem

DEAR MISS MANNERS:

My friend at work got fired for stealing money. Now she says maybe our friendship will grow stronger because we're not working together. My boss had me clean all of her stuff out of the office and put me in her place and is expecting me to do better than her. Also, my boss wants to know where my friend is working and what she is doing. How can I get out of the middle of this situation? It's becoming very stressful.

GENTLE READER:

Don't you want to get out of that friendship?

Miss Manners hates to discourage loyalty, and acknowledges that you might have noble reasons for strengthening your ties to your friend now that you know she is a thief. But it would make things simpler if you were disillusioned enough to distance yourself from the friend. Then you could simply tell the boss that you don't see her any more.

If you do see her, it would be even less seemly for you to discuss her. Your boss may be disappointed if you say, "I'm terribly sorry, but I can't talk about a friend," but Miss Manners suspects that—considering his recent experience—he would also be relieved to know that an employee firmly observes ethical standards.

DEAR MISS MANNERS:

What is the best way to politely handle a coworker who will be justifiably fired?

This person did nothing illegal; he was unable to perform the job, and after months of hearing defensive blame-shifting, the supervisors have had enough. The office is small, but part of a large organization. There is a good chance that the person in question will be moved elsewhere in the organization, and I may still have to deal with him on a regular basis.

I've worked with him for only a brief time and regard him as a light nuisance. He fancies himself a key player on the team and proves his "in" status by assuming a joking familiarity with the group—"lighthearted" insults that are not appropriate between casual acquaintances. I expect he will be surprised when the rest of us do not react in outrage to his dismissal or engage in whispered bad-mouthing of the bosses.

How can I convey condolences on his misfortune without taking his side? And how can I deflect future conversations in the cafeteria when he wants to publicly defame my department?

GENTLE READER:

Any sort of condolences will lead to complaints, Miss Manners is obliged to warn you. Fired employees do not generally harbor kind thoughts about the companies and bosses who fired them. But that is not to say that it is impossible to show kindness, even to the deservedly unemployed. Would it be stretching a point too far to say that you will miss him?

Okay, how about that you will miss his doing whatever it was that he didn't botch? Still coming up blank? Then go with wishing him luck in the future, and voicing the hope that he finds work that will take advantage of his talents. You needn't worry about specifying what those talents are. He will supply them.

Going Our Separate Ways

DEAR MISS MANNERS:

Is there a polite way to sever a business relationship that has an aspect of friendship to it?

For the last two years, I have been paying a woman to give me once-a-week private riding lessons. We hit it off nicely when we first met, as we have several things in common besides horses. But now, for two reasons, I'd like to "move on."

The first reason is that I feel I've gone just about as far as I can go under her instruction, and would like to employ a more demanding and precise instructor.

The second reason is touchier. Although we get along well, not only does this woman like to talk, she likes to talk about her personal problems, endlessly and in great detail. And she has plenty of problems to choose from: myriad health concerns, a crumbling marriage, troubled teenaged kids, fights with other clients, to name a few.

At first, I didn't mind chatting while getting the horse ready or cooling down after the lesson, but the lessons have now turned into near-marathon monologues on her part, with me making as few comments as possible. I view my lesson as the sole time in my week when I can put my problems aside and concentrate on the horse. Apparently she's come to view it as a time for her to unload.

I don't think it'd be right to just "disappear." I do like the woman, and if I just went elsewhere, she'd eventually find out through the grapevine. Also, I know that she's lost at least two other clients due to her excessive personal gab. Am I doing her a disservice by not telling her the truth? (I dread doing this, because I know how upset she gets over any criticism, real or perceived.)

I thought of using two instructors at once (not uncommon), but frankly, I've come to dread her lessons rather than anticipate them. Suggesting we get together for a drink and a chat isn't very feasible, as she lives nearly an hour away, I have small children, etc.

I'm sure other readers have had similar problems with hairdressers, house cleaners, and so on, and could use some advice on how to extricate oneself as painlessly as possible.

GENTLE READER:

Miss Manners has never believed that the heart-to-heart talk was the answer to everything, and would hardly recommend attempting one with someone known to nurse grievances and to do all the talking.

Besides, what outcome do you expect? She may promise to keep quiet, which would probably only postpone the problem and fail to address your need for more rigorous instruction. More likely from your description, she is going to be hurt and you will either find yourself trying to comfort her by staying on, or switching from being the confidant for her grievances to being a featured meanie in her outpourings to others.

You are not obliged to give a reason for switching your patronage from one businessperson to another, and should do so only when you think it is likely to be more helpful than you expect it to be here. To avoid this, start out by saying instead what you have enjoyed and appreciated and then thank her but announce that it is time for you to move on. If asked why, thank her again but reply, "Oh, it's just time."

DEAR MISS MANNERS:

What is a tactful way to deal with customers when you no longer want or need their business because of the numerous problems they cause?

We own a small but upscale lunch restaurant, which caters primarily to businesspeople. While most of our customers are fine, there is a small number of regular customers—various confused, demanding, and neurotic types—who simply go through life being a burden on those who have to deal with them. These include self-important types who make officious demands and parents who bring small, unruly children—much too young for a restaurant such as ours—who are a great disturbance to other customers with their screaming, who have scratched and damaged our tabletops with metal toys and completely trashed the area with food and spilled drinks. Never a word of apology or any effort to control them.

The list goes on. There was a time when I thought we had to tolerate anything because "the customer is always right." Having seen what some customers are capable of, I no longer feel this way. Is there any polite way of saying, in effect: "We really don't want you as a customer any more. We're patient, but you have crossed over the line and used up your welcome here. Please go somewhere else."

GENTLE READER:

Must we part with that dictum that the customer is always right? Miss Manners is not so naïve as to believe it is the guiding principle of modern commerce, but she would like to keep alive the idea that it is a good thing not to let outrageous customers push trained servicepeople into retaliatory rudeness.

This doesn't mean you, she hastens to add. You have a reasonable position and want to exercise tact. So perhaps we could agree that some of your customers might be—shall we say, more right?—elsewhere.

The technique you need is known in private schools (where the intention is to avoid hurting a child who will never be able to keep up with the academic standards of the school) as "counseling them out." The approach is: We have your best interests at heart and believe you would be happier elsewhere.

In this case, you say, in reference to the telephone service or protection of a child on the loose, "I'm afraid we really don't have the facilities here to take care of your needs. We will be sorry to lose your business, but we understand that other restaurants would be more suitable for you."

DEAR MISS MANNERS:

We love our family dentist but he is so booked all the time it's hard to get an appointment in the same year with him. He recently went into partnership with a new dentist who is still building up his clientele and the new guy did some work on my daughter's teeth and we really like him, too.

Our dentist seems like a family friend to us, and I really don't want to hurt his feelings by taking our business to his partner. I have often wondered this same thing in other family practice situations. Is it considered rude to switch from one doctor to another in the same practice? Is there a proper way of doing this?

GENTLE READER:

Business is business, and one should be able to thank one professional and move on to another. Yet Miss Manners often hears from ladies who have sacrificed their satisfaction with their own hair for fear of devastating their hairdressers by moving on. She has always wondered if they exhibit the same delicacy toward unsatisfactory husbands.

You don't really have a problem. Your dentist should be pleased to hear that you like his new partner, and that you are seeing him because you know your friend is overbooked. At least if you put it that way, he will have to seem so.

Letting Go

In case of firing, panic causes damage. And that applies to bystanders as well as to those whose hopes have gone up in flames.

Miss Manners is often told by someone who wanted to offer sympathy that "I just didn't know what to say," and nothing good ever follows. That may be an admission of having said nothing, which amounts to shunning and adds to the devastation. Or the would-be comforter makes things worse by trying to make them sound better:

"You're better off—we have to stay, and now we'll all have extra work."

"Don't worry, you'll find something."

"You probably knew this was coming."

"Stay in touch. We'll have lunch, okay?"

That last one would be all right if a specific date were proposed, and even better if job contacts can be brought to that lunch. But even if no practical help can be offered, it is essential to show that the victim is not so badly scarred for life that no one can bear to look at him. The least soon-to-be-former colleagues can do at the time is to say, "Rotten luck."

DEAR MISS MANNERS:

After 19 years' service, two years away from retirement, I was fired. My immediate supervisor did not step forward to assume responsibility or blame regarding a few issues contributing to this termination. For example: I was accused of failure to complete subordinates' accident reports, when in fact I did turn them in to him but watched helpless as he tossed them, saying, "Higher-ups do not need this information."

I lost my job, my house, my car. I stay with friends and family—a day here, a day there.

A letter from my supervisor's wife was forwarded to me, stating that he tells her that he thinks we worked well together and misses me. Too bad for me that I cannot find other employment and became too busy to even consider a reply.

What shall I do? "Nothing" is not an option for me. I hate loose ends. Please be gentle with this Gentle Reader. My self-esteem is in the gutter.

GENTLE READER:

Miss Manners suggests you fish it out. You have no cause for shame and you don't want to wallow in the gutter with your former supervisor, who does and is.

He has been moping about this so much that his wife is trying to make amends with you, in the hope that this will assuage his conscience. She figures that if she gets a nice letter back (perhaps because you might need him as a reference), she can use it to argue that as you don't hold his behavior against him, there is no reason for him to do so.

What neither she nor you realizes is that the letter you would prefer to write would be an even bigger help to them. No show of hostility, however carefully worded, would strike them as deserved. Rather, it would convince them that there is something unpleasant about you that justified the firing, and that his failings had nothing to do with that, after all.

Does doing nothing (in the etiquette line, whatever else you may do legally) begin to sound better to you? This person's self-esteem is in the gutter and all you need to do is to refrain from helping him fish it out.

DEAR MISS MANNERS:

My new boyfriend was recently released from our company. My company picnic is coming up and I would like to ask him to go. The company is under 60 people and we have not been dating very long; very few people in the office know. I am afraid this would be awkward. Any advice?

GENTLE READER:

Spare him.

DEAR MISS MANNERS:

What is one's social obligation to disgruntled former employees?

Until recently, I was chairman of a church board which forced out a long-term employee. Today, I received a short, hostile note critiquing my letter advising her that we had voted not to renew her contract, and my letter of recommendation.

I sent both my letters over six months ago, when the events occurred. They were pleasant and diplomatic, stressing her strengths and long service. They made no mention—direct or hidden—of how she antagonized many people in her last years of employment.

I think her gestures and the note were intended to hurt and insult me. Instead, I was surprised and somewhat at a loss for action.

She had had a comparable job for several months—taking the immediacy out of returning my reference. Before she left, I made it plain, repeatedly, that I respected what she had accomplished, but that the position had changed and needed a different set of skills. She apparently will not accept that, and remains hurt and angry.

It seems any contact from me angers her still, and I don't feel I should respond to her note. Yet I regret that she is still holding onto this. Should I mention this to one of the volunteers she will still speak to, or let it go? It's a shame she won't view her service for its many virtues and accept earned praise. I would like her to have that.

GENTLE READER:

Miss Manners advises you to let it go. While you seem to have been meticulously fair, even generous, in your handling of the matter, and the lady in question is foolish to launch a counterattack, even from the safety of another job, let it go.

The fact is that you cannot expect to be loved by someone you have fired. You remind Miss Manners of the kindly souls who inquire how to end a romance without making the other person "feel rejected."

QUITTING

DEAR MISS MANNERS:

It seems like an employer who asks a question expects an honest answer.

Here's the thing. After several years with an organization I didn't care for, I got an offer for a new job—at higher pay and with responsibilities that seem more in line with my skills. I have given several weeks of notice. This employer has a practice—one of many busy-work functions designed by its human resource department to justify its own existence—of asking departing staff to complete an exit interview that will ask about the reasons we're leaving.

I harbor no ill will toward any specific individuals. In fact, I have a decent relationship with my boss. But I can't help but savor the opportunity to give a truthful assessment of why I was anxious to leave: I found the organization's culture self-congratulatory, bloated, inflexible, and unappreciative.

In my heart, I know that living well is the best revenge. But if they go through the trouble of asking why I'm leaving, am I at liberty to give an honest assessment? Or should I consider this letter to you my chance to vent?

Alternatively, do I simply hand back a blank survey? That also seems rude. But I really don't feel like investing the time to go into detail describing my notion of the problems. If they ever seemed to care, I might not have been so anxious to leave.

GENTLE READER:

Come, now. Over those years, your employer asked you lots of honest questions: "Are you going to have this in by Thursday?" "Do you agree with my idea?" "Do you mind staying late?" and so on.

You did not give dishonest answers, Miss Manners trusts. But you phrased things in such a way as to avoid antagonizing management: "I'll try my best, but it's more complicated than we had thought." "It's a great idea, but I have a couple of suggestions." "Of course not, but unfortunately, tonight . . ."

But now that you are leaving, you want to give it to them straight. Don't. These people are in your field. You are only too likely to encounter them again. Your reason should be that you found a better position and salary.

DEAR MISS MANNERS:

I recently accepted a position at a new firm and have been working there for a couple of weeks. To my dismay, I am slowly learning that I may not be the ideal fit that I once thought I would be. However, I do not want to leave immediately, as I view that as very unprofessional (I was at my previous firm for over 5 years). What is a recommended minimum length of stay for an employee before I could leave on good terms, and how can I phrase it to my employer so I don't seem like I'm a quitter?

GENTLE READER:

Miss Manners supposes she should be flattered at the amount of faith in etiquette that your question demonstrates. All she has to do is to devise some polite phrasing that will enable you to quit without appearing to be a quitter. Suppose it works. What would your boss think when he didn't see you around any longer? That if he waited long enough, you'd come out of the restroom?

All right, all right, Miss Manners will give it a try. Let's see—how about some pungent phrases that will make your employer fire you? No? Then let's work with your own words, throwing in a few nice ones of Miss Manners' devising: "I'm in a peculiar position here. It's a great place to work, but I realize that I'm not the ideal fit for this job. In fairness to us both, I've decided to leave sooner rather than later. It's a shame, because I've enjoyed it, but I've given it a lot of thought, and I know it's the right thing to do."

The time to leave is before the employer starts wondering how he should phrase the idea.

DEAR MISS MANNERS:

I no longer enjoy my job and am currently looking for employment elsewhere. However, because I hate my job, due in very large part to my coworkers, I may give my notice before I have a different job.

Considering I do the lion's share of the work in my department, and everyone makes light comments about how the other girl always gets out of working (Ha ha isn't that hilarious), I just know I may have to give my two weeks one day when I simply have had enough!

The problem is that from the time I resign until I finally walk out for the last time, everyone will want to know why and also what I will be doing.

If I have a job, it's no problem. But if not, I am afraid I'll say something very true that will also be rude. So, I was wondering if you could suggest some answer that is polite and that I can practice so that I don't say it in the tone I'm probably thinking it in.

GENTLE READER:

Good; let's work on tone.

What you will have to say is, "I haven't quite decided" or "I can't talk about it yet." But Miss Manners can hear the tone in your head: a fine mixture of bitterness, anger, and self-pity conveying, "All right, you horrid people, you've driven me away, and I don't even know where my next job is coming from."

As you have guessed, this will not shame them. It will only make them decide that you had "problems"—meaning other than themselves.

The tone you need to develop is one of barely suppressed excitement and satisfaction. You might practice saying the necessary statements while thinking how you would say it if you had a White House appointment that you were not allowed to discuss before the president announced it.

RETIRING

DEAR MISS MANNERS:

Having witnessed many job departures—whether for retirement or to a new job location—in my military career and since then in civilian life, I know they can be done poorly. To illustrate the point:

At a small lunch to bid farewell to a popular N.C.O., she stood up to acknowledge the gifts and warm farewell sentiments and said, "I'm leaving and never coming back." Then she sat down.

Admittedly, this woman had had some difficulties at this location, with her children's school and illnesses, but this less than gracious goodbye left the audience feeling short-changed on the niceties, if not outright insulted because their friendship (not to mention gifts and time and effort to honor her) were not acknowledged.

Another departing employee specified that her farewell lunch must be kept small, otherwise she would not come. Her boss honored her ultimatum—it was not a request—and those of us who wanted to say goodbye properly were denied the opportunity.

This had the effect of making me, for one, want to say, "Good riddance." Surely Miss Manners could have supplied the precisely proper words to bid farewell while subtly conveying an acerbic opinion of this selfish behavior.

At last a happy story: When a friend retiring from the Air Force told his boss that he wanted no ceremony—just give him the paperwork and let him walk out the door—my wife begged him to have a ceremony. She understands that this provides a fitting and rewarding end to a career.

My friend's boss talked him into it, and the event exuded warmth and sentiment. My wife and I also hosted a small retirement dinner for the couple, which they appreciated greatly, and he admitted that he was glad he had been coerced into the ceremony. He now understood how fitting it was.

The common thread here concerns expectations of guests and obligations and rewards of the honorees at these ritual functions, but I cannot quite put my finger on it.

GENTLE READER:

It is that people have become embarrassed at the idea of ceremony, because it doesn't seem to have a direct practical justification, and because it purports to be solemn in a world that prides itself on being jokey and detached.

Even weddings, celebrated more fervently than ever, try to introduce entertainment into the ceremony, as do funerals, when they are not minimized or avoided.

Whether one undercuts the ceremony with modesty, as was attempted by your friend who tried to squelch the idea of marking his retirement, or with sarcasm, as did the N.C.O., who took the opportunity to insult her colleagues, the result is to belittle the occasion. The attitude that the ceremony is purely for the benefit of its central figure, while the feelings of others with an interest in the event don't count, doesn't help either.

We still desperately need ritual to mark the milestones of life, filled as they are with difficult and contradictory emotions. The beauty and comfort of knowing that one is part of a social tradition and surrounded by people who care is overthrown at one's peril.

DEAR MISS MANNERS:

My husband's retirement comes in a few months, and already close friends are asking me for gift ideas as well as whether there will be any festivity to celebrate the occasion. While there will be a reception at the office, it is for coworkers and families only.

I feel that my hosting my husband's retirement party might be like the mother of the bride holding her daughter's shower. Our children have the financial burdens all young people raising family have, and I don't feel it should be on them to come up with a party.

GENTLE READER:

It's not actually "on" anyone. If your husband's friends want to celebrate his retirement surely they should think of giving him a party.

Not that you are banned from giving one if you want to do so. Spouses are allowed to give one another an occasional party—very occasional. Say three a lifetime. A thirtieth and a sixtieth birthday party (or other well-spaced combination, such as fiftieth and eighty-fifth) and perhaps one for a prize promotion or retirement.

But Miss Manners appreciates your delicacy about the aspect that seems to encourage presents for a member of one's own family. The best way to get around that is merely to invite people to a party, and then offer a toast for the occasion once they are there, giving them the chance to protest that they wish they had known so they could have brought a present.

In this case, it might be charming to issue invitations not to honor him, but "to celebrate our having more leisure now to spend with our friends."

DEAR MISS MANNERS:

We now have the all-time low in tasteless retirement/going-away gifts. I saw a very masculine gentleman "honored" for 25 years of service with a certificate for a facial and massage at a day spa. Our very conservative minister was given a karaoke machine to honor his years of service.

Whatever happened to the idea that these kinds of gifts should be silver, porcelain, or crystal, designed to last two lifetimes?

GENTLE READER:

Oddly enough, what sometimes happens is that the standard corporate present has been dropped in favor of something intended to be more personal. Yet that attempt, so charming in private life, can be disastrous in professional life, where the individual's taste may not be known—or may be a vanity that is known but that the recipient may not be thrilled to have publicly revealed.

Miss Manners' other, perhaps shrewder, guess is that these people are being given whatever happens to be available free, regardless of its suitability.

EXIT CEREMONIES

DEAR MISS MANNERS:

I will soon be faced with the challenge of announcing the resignation of one of my key employees. Since I neither "regret" nor am "deeply saddened" by her decision to leave, what opening line would be appropriate to use in my letter to the staff?

GENTLE READER:

There are plenty of conventional phrases left for you to use without resorting to those. Miss Manners suggests quickly following the statement that this person "will be leaving us soon" with lots of warmth and enthusiasm about how you wish her well in her new career.

Parting Partying

DEAR MISS MANNERS:

I recently quit a job where I was disliked by both coworkers and supervisors, but I was still offered a going-away party. I declined, thinking it would be in bad taste to celebrate a departure that would be welcomed by all. I was told I was being "ungracious" to refuse. Who was right?

GENTLE READER:

Miss Manners thinks you were quite right to refuse to participate in the charade of regretful departure. Surely your disappointed colleagues are free to celebrate now that you are gone.

DEAR MISS MANNERS:

The department in which I work is quite large and employees' salaries range from minimum wage to doctorate. A large percentage of people are longtime workers, but with cutbacks and reconstructions, we are seeing more and more part-time and per-diem people. People seem to come and go at rates that range from a few weeks to thirty years.

And when someone leaves there is always someone who passes the hat or card or envelope to "collect" to get this someone a parting gift. I have no problem with this as most of these people were friends.

But lately the collector is listing the dollar amount on the envelope with your name following. This way he or she allows everyone to see just how much the person gave. We even have collectors setting the amount to give so that they can be certain to collect the needed funds for a preselected gift they have in mind.

It's fine for me to put the ten-dollar bill in the envelope, but what about the file clerk and receptionist whose ten-dollar bill could mean the difference between lunch and no lunch? Am I overreacting to find this practice annoying?

GENTLE READER:

Your department sounds like a wonderful place to leave. The departing employee not only receives a present, but escapes being the victim of extortion and humiliation.

Miss Manners appreciates your concern for those who are bullied out of their lunch money, but surely the principle is the same regardless of ability to pay. Someone ought to be going around the department taking names, all right, but on a petition to end this travesty of sociability.

Losing Touch

DEAR MISS MANNERS:

On my last day of work after quitting my job, several coworkers I was friendly with gave me cards with their phone numbers and urged me to call so we could go out some time.

I understand that "Let's go out some time" often means "Let's not go out and say we did." However, these coworkers kept insisting. I was flattered.

Two days after my last day of work, one of them called me and we had a pleasant conversation until I asked if she would like to have coffee the next day. She hesitated, agreed unenthusiastically, and got off the phone so quickly I barely had a chance to say goodbye.

She never called, we never met for coffee, and when I saw her a week later, she claimed to have lost my number and asked me to call her. I decided to give her the benefit of the doubt and left a message on her answering machine the next day, but she never called back.

Am I misunderstanding? When they insist on getting together and even call me, does this actually mean, "I want to talk to you on the phone, but I don't want to go on social outings with you"? I hate trying to read minds. When I see these people, do I nod politely and walk on by, or must I stop and talk to them?

GENTLE READER:

The misleading thing about workplace friendships is that they almost never are. Like many a workplace romance, they tend to become emotionally inflated by daily proximity and shared experience.

Miss Manners doesn't mean to suggest that your former coworkers didn't like you and genuinely want to keep in touch. Had you suggested coffee some months later, you would probably have been met with enthusiasm.

But by popping up right away, you seem to be hanging on as a member of the workforce even though you will no longer have the same interests and information. Yet it is too early for there to be any interesting catching-up to do on their lives and yours.

She suggests leaving your coffee with old friends or new colleagues for a while. Later on, your old colleagues will be delighted to catch you up on all you will have missed.

DEAR MISS MANNERS:

Upon learning that I had found a new job, a former boss sent me a congratulatory note that included the phrase, "We miss you here."

I would have welcomed this sentiment, except that she was the one who had terminated my prior employment. So far I've been a good sport about her power-play-disguised-as-layoffs. Must I continue to hold my tongue?

GENTLE READER:

Have you considered the possibility that your former boss does miss you, regrets having let you go, and is paving the way for some day wooing you back?

Miss Manners can hardly think of a more satisfactory impression for a terminated employee to leave. "They'll miss me when I'm gone" is surely the fantasy of everyone who feels unfairly treated.

However, you can probably fix that, as well as any chance of your needing her recommendation or wanting to work there ever again. An unleashed stream of rudeness would be a comfortable reminder that she no longer has to deal with you.

Part 2

The Long Haul—On the Job

CHAPTER 3

What's That You Say?

DEAR MISS MANNERS:

What is your take on gender-specific job titles?

I work as a flight attendant, and my skin crawls when I am called a "stewardess." One reason is because I don't think my sex should affect my job title and my ability to perform my job. Also it conjures images up of actual work rules that affected "stewardesses" (as called by the airlines before it was changed to "flight attendants" in the 1970s) such as weight restrictions, marital status, and sex.

I try to understand that many people are older and when they did fly last it may have been in the 1980s, or that they come from smaller towns where gender-specific language is not considered offensive. I try not to be sensitive to it but I am. I have heard the same complaint from "male nurses." A nurse should be called a nurse regardless of his or her sex. Right?

GENTLE READER:

Brace yourself. Many not born in the 1980s now glamorize the era when airlines considered the youth, beauty, and even presumed availability of those in your profession to be a major selling point.

Miss Manners finds the larger question of masculine and feminine endings in job descriptions more complicated than you do. Job titles that included the word "man" absolutely had to be changed or given female equivalents, she acknowledges. "Fireman" to "firefighter," for example, or "congressman" and "congresswoman." And she agrees with your friends the nurses that titles that do not specify gender need not have that added.

But in jobs that have traditionally been filled by both genders, she finds it unfortunate that the masculine version is being adopted for all. Actresses now call themselves actors, as if that designation were somehow more serious. Yet there have been serious actresses for several centuries now.

Passenger ships have long had both stewards and stewardesses, without a derogatory connotation becoming attached to the latter. Perhaps your passengers who have not flown in decades were taking ships. Miss Manners would advise you not to take their words amiss. However, those who use a lascivious tone when calling you a stewardess should be favored with the frosty look that is the proper response to any lasciviousness toward working people.

DEAR MISS MANNERS:

In my workplace, everyone has a job title. They are very specific, and leave no room for speculation as to who is at the bottom of the heap and who is at the top. Let's say my job title is "Widget Polisher I." My direct supervisor, whose job title is, say, "Technical Widget Polisher IV," introduces me to job seekers, people touring the plant, and even her personal friends, as "Joyce . . . our 'Widget Polisher I.'" This has gone on for years.

Am I wrong to be irritated? These titles are meaningless to the general public, and seem to me to have no place in a polite introduction.

GENTLE READER:

Miss Manners has long supported those who resent having their social identities merged with their job descriptions, so that people collected merely to socialize are immediately informed of one another's occupations. But she is not about to get involved in objecting to job titles being used on the job. People who are in the plant, being told what is done there, are legitimately interested in the tasks of those they meet.

If you feel the titles are demeaning, that is another matter, and should be taken up as a matter of company policy. Personally, Miss Manners thinks the ones you told her are charming.

Honorifics

DEAR MISS MANNERS:

As a new business owner, I find I am troubled with how to address my customers. Many times I feel comfortable in addressing them by their first name in lieu of Mr. or Mrs. So-and-So.

But even though I am comfortable with this first-name basis, many customers may not be. Is there a correct way to handle this, or should I just refer to everyone as Mr., Mrs., Miss, or Ms.?

GENTLE READER:

What do you mean, "or"? That is the correct way to address people with whom you have a business relationship.

Miss Manners is sorry to be so hoity-toity, but she has not heard of customers being overly preoccupied with the comfort level of the people with whom they do business. However, she has heard of their interest in being treated with respect. You may drop the honorifics only when those being addressed request you to do so.

DEAR MISS MANNERS:

I am 23 years old, and I get very offended when salespersons and clerks address me as "Ma'am." Am I correct in my assumption that it would be more appropriate to address me as "Miss," as I am unmarried, have no children, and am under the age of 30? Is it appropriate for me to gently correct such offenders?

GENTLE READER:

Is it appropriate for Miss Manners to put her head down on the table and weep?

Dear lady (unless you would rather be called a girl), women have spent the better part of this century struggling to be treated with respect, to be valued for something other than their youth, and not to be classified by their marital status. And you are proposing going around teaching people the opposite.

Fortunately, chastising people who are obviously only trying to treat you with courtesy is not allowed by the rules of etiquette. So you are barred from delivering reprimands that would ruin things for the rest of us. Miss Manners suggests that you learn to accept and enjoy such a respectful title as "Ma'am." There are a lot worse alternatives around.

DEAR MISS MANNERS:

I have a job in a scientific organization at a fairly high level. Most people who have attained this level are PhDs. I am not, but frequently find myself being introduced as Dr.

What is the most gracious way of correcting people? In some situations, such as a speaker or at international forums, it may be impossible, but in others it might be appropriate. In correspondence, this is easier to right.

GENTLE READER:

Unfortunately, you can't go around saying, "I don't have a PhD." Miss Manners cannot explain why it seems as boastful to brag about not having a degree as it is to brag about having one, but such is the case.

In correspondence you can use the title "Ms." as you did in the return address, or in parentheses beneath your signature. Beyond that, you can only say quietly to those likely to repeat the mistake, "Oh, by the way, it's 'Ms. Worthington,' not 'Dr. Worthington.'" That this may lead some to believe that you not only have a PhD but are modest and confident enough to refrain from using the title is neither your problem nor Miss Manners' fault.

Coworkers and Employees, Boys and Girls

DEAR MISS MANNERS:

Should a manager refer to the people who work for him/her as his/her "coworkers" or "employees"?

GENTLE READER:

Miss Manners sees the problem: "employees" seems to rub in the inequality, while "coworkers" achieves the same effect by coyly denying it. Nevertheless, she does not care for the choice. Let's try "staff." Miss Manners trusts that people associate this word more with competence than with infections.

DEAR MISS MANNERS:

It is clear that you believe that it was never correct to refer to an adult employee as a "girl." However, I am unable to find any suggestion as to how the manager might refer to the female office employee.

As a retired educational administrator, I do not recall female office employees referred to, even by themselves, as "office women," "office ladies," or anything else other than "office girls." As examples: "We girls went out to lunch." "We girls stopped for a drink after work." "We girls are going to the theater." "We girls are giving a shower for the bride-to-be."

Yes, I have heard of the "Ladies' Aid," the "women's club," and the American Association of University Women. But from adult women, including those who admit to being "senior citizens" or "older adults," in referring to their peers I most frequently hear them use the word "girls." "We girls played bridge." "We girls"—all widows from the adult mobile home park—"went out to dinner."

So I ask: What is the hang-up with regard to the use of the word "girls" in referring to adult women? It can still be done respectfully. And yes, I have heard adult men refer to "going out with the boys" when I was certain they did not mean with their sons and/or grandsons.

GENTLE READER:

Miss Manners finds it curious that although your question is about how an office manager should refer to workers, your examples all illustrate what people call themselves, and in situations that are social in character.

There is no example of a female secretary asking, "Do you boys want your letters done now?" or the shop steward announcing, "The girls are demanding a raise."

You are correct that Miss Manners believes in adults being identified as such. But she also recognizes that people are allowed more leeway in what they call themselves than in what they call others; that socializing, even in a casual, coffee-break type of way, lends itself to informality of speech; and that older generations are used to different terminology than younger ones.

Regardless of the fact that you seem to have been getting away with using the nearly archaic terms that you have heard some workers calling themselves when discussing their off-duty socializing, you office boys must stop taking verbal liberties with the staff. One of these days you will get into trouble over it.

Anyway, it is not necessary to refer to any group of office workers by gender, unless dealing with a class action they have brought. Refer to them by their jobs—"the computer programmers," "second-level management"—even if they happen to be all of the same gender. Calling attention to that will get you into even more serious personnel problems.

Who Ya Talkin' To?

DEAR MISS MANNERS:

I'm a female executive who travels to Europe frequently on business. On a recent trip to Scandinavia, two colleagues and I met with a new business partner we'll be working closely with. Despite the fact that he knew I was the project leader, he insisted on addressing my junior male colleague and rarely met my eye. Even after my colleague reminded him that I was heading up the project, he continued this annoying tendency. I have another meeting with this guy soon. How can I get him to knock off his sexist and disrespectful behavior?

GENTLE READER:

Just when Miss Manners is convinced that business has become so ruthless that people will do anything to get ahead, she hears about someone's sabotaging his own interest by unnecessarily antagonizing a high-ranking person.

Snubbing people on the basis of gender, race, or because that person is in a wheelchair is never a good idea, but it is especially unwise to do this to the person in charge. Too bad Miss Manners cannot take comfort from discovering that prejudice is stronger than ambition.

Your junior colleague can be of help, but not by speaking up for you. That only confirms the impression that he is in charge. At your next meeting, tell your new partner that you want your junior colleague to work out some points with someone of junior rank on his staff while you two tend to more substantive matters.

DEAR MISS MANNERS:

At a long meeting, my boss twice referred to a business associate, with whom we were engaging in a joint venture, by the wrong name. Our associate did not correct him, but seemed perplexed at the error.

I considered doing nothing and leaving it to the two of them to work out. I considered passing my boss a note, but that would have been rather obvious under the circumstances. I chose, instead, to take the next opportunity to address our associate by his correct name.

Although my boss began to use the proper name, later apologized for his error, and did not seem to be angry with me, I am still wondering if I took the correct action—if, indeed, any action was appropriate. No doubt, Miss Manners would have been more sure of herself.

GENTLE READER:

Well, yes, Miss Manners is nothing if not sure of herself. She would have done exactly what you did, except that she would have omitted worrying about it.

It is a kindness to stop someone from repeating an error (not to mention wisdom to rescue a boss from looking bad), but essential that this be done discreetly. As the idea is to save embarrassment, it should not be done by causing more.

Shake on It?

DEAR MISS MANNERS:

Being an older female executive, I am in contact with representatives of insurance companies, bankers, salesmen, etc., who are 20 to 30 years my junior. When we meet for our appointments in my office, they offer their hands to shake mine. If I am seated at my desk, do I stand to shake hands, or remain seated? If I happen to be standing when they walk in, it presents no problem.

GENTLE READER:

My, we have a lot of factors to play with here: age, rank, gender, and, finally, venue. A lady doesn't rise for a gentleman; older people do not rise for younger; and higher-ranking people do not rise for lower-ranking people. But—it is your office, and they are visitors. Therefore, you do rise, as hostess, so to speak.

All of the above conditions (except possibly that of gender, which is the least important in an office situation and can even be ignored, although it would be a key factor in social life, where business rank is ignored) dictate that you should be the first to offer to shake hands. However, these juniors mean well in their ignorance, and it is a marked rudeness to refuse to shake a proffered hand, so you and Miss Manners will overlook the transgression.

DEAR MISS MANNERS:

I am male, aged 27, and a software engineer. My religion prohibits me from making physical contact with members of the opposite sex (except family members).

Now, in my day-to-day work, I sometimes have to meet female clients. When being introduced, I politely nod and do not offer a hand, with the hope it will be understood. However, sometimes the client offers her handshake, and I have to respond in order not to offend her. I do not like to do this because it compromises my religious values that I hold strongly. How do I tackle this problem?

GENTLE READER:

Not by compromising your religious values, Miss Manners assures you, but neither by assuming that this will be understood. You are living in a country where the handshake is considered to be an impersonal show of good will and the refusal to shake hands a high insult. At that, you're lucky not to be in one of the subcultures that considers a kiss to be an impersonal show of good will.

As with people speaking different languages, you not only need to translate when you are speaking a language that you presume to be unknown to your listeners, but to make sure that your intent is not misunderstood. Yet you certainly don't want to open a religious discussion every time you meet someone, and certainly not with clients.

Miss Manners suggests saying only, "Sorry I can't shake hands," perhaps offering a friendly little half-wave to demonstrate good will. There are many reasons people don't shake hands, and whether your clients realize this is a religious matter or assume it has to do with an injury doesn't matter. You can head off inquiries by jumping in and saying, "But I'm delighted to see you," and then opening the matter you are meeting to discuss.

THE WRITTEN WORD

DEAR MISS MANNERS:

I use my given name, Patricia, on my business cards, name tags, etc., but I prefer to be called by my nickname, Pat. In business situations, should I have "(Pat)" printed on my cards? I do try to have my nickname used on temporary name tags, such as at meetings and conferences.

GENTLE READER:

In an ideal world, you would have your formal name printed on your card and people would address you using only your surname with a title until you said, charmingly, "Oh, please call me Pat." But you're not in the ideal world; you're in the modern business world. People are probably going to call you whatever first name they read on the card. Perhaps "Hi, Patricia (Pat), how ya doing?"

So it is just as well that you put only "Pat" on name tags, as that is how you prefer to be addressed. A way to preserve your formal name on your cards—and offer a semblance of the aforementioned charm—would be to draw a line through "Patricia" before you hand one over, writing "Pat" there instead.

Oops

DEAR MISS MANNERS:

I am mystified at how to respond to the accidental insults that slips of the finger on keyboard make possible, now that technology has opened vast new vistas for rudeness.

I was the recipient of an email message addressed to me, but obviously, from its content, meant for someone else. In it, the sender vented considerable spleen about—me.

Since I have to work with this woman, I decided not to mention it, but somehow she discovered what she had done. Another missive immediately arrived, which began as an apology, but ended up a justification of her opinions as expressed in the misdirected communication. In essence, a compounding of the initial insult.

How does the polite technophile respond to such provocation, considering that it is impossible to cut someone dead with a withering stare via computer?

GENTLE READER:

No, it's not. Miss Manners assures you that these things just need a bit of updating to fit the technology.

In conventional correspondence, the equivalent of the cut is to return a letter unopened. In the case of email, the idea that you didn't open it is not convincing. But if you add at the top "I trust this was not intended for me," you can, with a simple touch of the button, return to, and incidentally frustrate and annoy, an offensive sender.

DEAR MISS MANNERS:

My boss has a tendency to send me notes in email that are all CAPS. This drives me crazy because I think she's always yelling at me. I don't think she intends to shout instructions over the computer to me but that's what it feels like. How do I ask her to turn off the flame without embarrassing her or inflaming her?

GENTLE READER:

As you rightly assume, there is no polite way to tell your boss to pipe down. But saving her from her own ignorance is, if deftly done, an employee's duty.

At least for the moment, most bosses are not embarrassed by receiving gentle instructions from their subordinates on computer usage. They know small children who are far cleverer at the computer than they can ever hope to be, and thus do not associate this skill with being in charge.

So Miss Manners thinks it unlikely to be dangerous if you say politely, "It always alarms me when I get your messages all in caps, because that's the computer equivalent of yelling. Do you mean to be sending them that way?"

The answer will either be, "No, of course not," which will solve your problem, or "You'd better believe I do," which will at least make clear what your real problem is.

DEAR MISS MANNERS:

I have a colleague who consistently forgets to include attachments to email messages. How do I politely reply to this person and request that they resend the message with the attachment?

GENTLE READER:

Yes, between those people and the ones who send attachments that can't be opened by the recipients, or attachments that take forever to open and are not worth it, we are all going mad. Yet Miss Manners urges patience and a polite reply of "Please resend attachment." Manners alone mandate this, but forgoing snapping back will protect you against counter-snaps on the inevitable day when you forget to attach an attachment.

DEAR MISS MANNERS:

Is there a polite way to tell my boss that "thx" instead of "thank you" or even "thanks" at the end of an email kind of defeats the purpose? Thx.

GENTLE READER:

Yr wlcm. And it is going to get worse as written English twitters away. Miss Manners is sorry to have to tell you that you are bound by the rule against criticizing others, and the likely consequences of criticizing your boss.

Reply All

DEAR MISS MANNERS:

I'm puzzled by how often people ignore email messages when they would never fail to reply to the same request transmitted by paper, phone, or in person. (I hasten to add that by email I don't mean spam, forwarded jokes, chain letters, or other junk but ordinary, brief, to-the-point business or personal messages.)

Is it simply that most of us are so buried in email that we can't FIND the real stuff, or is there some secret email etiquette I don't know about? People often cheerfully acknowledge getting a message from me but don't seem the least abashed about not replying.

Do I really have to go back to paper memos, phone calls, and hovering in people's doorways to have a hope of getting a reply? Email seems so efficient, but not if it's ignored!

GENTLE READER:

As we have all discovered by now, the problem with email, as well as its great advantage, is its efficiency. So everyone uses it to convey every little passing observation to everyone else.

That is all very well for those who want to keep expressing themselves, but the result to the recipient, even aside from the spam and junk, is as if everyone one knows is talking all at once. Of course one should sort email in terms of what needs attention when, but that is no sooner done than another load of messages arrives.

As you have noticed, some people just give up. So yes, Miss Manners is afraid that when you need an immediate reply, you will have to hope that they have not turned off their telephones and deserted their offices to work at home.

DEAR MISS MANNERS:

Lately, I have been receiving cards from companies thanking me for my business and from associates thanking me for a referral and other types of business courtesies. What do you think of this trend? Should I be doing it, too?

GENTLE READER:

Do you send out all the thank-you letters that you owe to friends and relations who have given you presents, entertained you at dinner parties or overnight, or done you any special favors? Truthfully?

If so, Miss Manners will at least not discourage you from writing thank-you letters to business associates. She does not want to condemn courtesy in any form, but finds it odd that the hope of profit is giving new life to a custom that the incentive of pleasing friends had not prevented from falling into disuse.

THE SPOKEN WORD

DEAR MISS MANNERS:

I am a receptionist at a very large stock brokerage house and supposedly these are professional businesspeople. You would not believe how they act, talk, curse, and just carry on when they are on the telephone.

I get screamed at constantly. I have had to tell them to lower their voice because I can hear perfectly, plus most telephones have speakers that make your voice louder. If you knew the number of ear infections we get because people think they have to scream at the top of their lungs you would be amazed.

Rude, nasty people! At times I can almost imagine the venom dripping from their mouths. I have been cursed at and insulted in God knows how many languages because I could not understand what they were saying. Now mind you, I am not supposed to say anything to defend myself because I could be fired instantly.

And slamming the telephone down in your ear when you have spent precious time telling them that the line is busy or the person they are calling isn't even in the office. And the chewing gum, coughing, hacking, sneezing, or talking to someone in the background and telling me to shut up. Well, hang up and finish your conversation. Remember you called us—I didn't call you.

As you can probably guess, this has been driving me wild for quite some time. I have been employed as a Receptionist/Front Desk/Switchboard Operator for about 20 years so I did not just take this job yesterday. I have received many compliments and acknowledgments for my work over the years and just cannot believe how people get away with this conduct without realizing that they don't want to be treated like dirt but it is natural for them to treat the person answering the telephone as such. They just don't know the meaning of the word "manners."

GENTLE READER:

No, they don't, and you are overdue for a vacation. Miss Manners believes it would be in the interests of business to seek out those who have managed to refrain from returning public rudeness with rudeness of their own, and give them a well-deserved break before they crack.

The Misspoken Word

DEAR MISS MANNERS:

I am a telesurveyor (we do not sell anything) and have been making calls to the USA recently. The people in the East Coast and Southern states do not have a clue how to be polite on the phone or use proper phone etiquette.

I realize the nature of the business causes people to be upset and irascible, but in the States the people use such vulgarities and rudeness. However, as soon as I make calls up north the disposition and demeanor changes 180 degrees. Why such a difference? I know Canadians are always referred to as being polite. Is that really such a bad "handle"?

GENTLE READER:

Being polite is always good, Miss Manners assures you. She just hopes you realize that it is not polite to telephone strangers at home when they have shown no interest in hearing from you.

This is no excuse for their being vulgar or rude in return, she agrees. But neither are they obliged to hear you out. She hopes that you are not counting it as rude when people simply terminate the call by saying that they are not interested.

DEAR MISS MANNERS:

I'm afraid I've been rude, and I'm looking for forgiveness. As a professional woman, I've had to put up with years of people assuming I must be the secretary, asking me to get them coffee, and asking to speak to "someone with authority" as if that couldn't possibly be me.

Today, it happened one too many times. A company representative making a cold call to sell his products to my firm was referred to me. I answered my phone "Mary Smith," as I always do, and he proceeded: "Mary, this is Mr. Jones with the ABC Company, I'd like to speak to someone . . ."

Seething, I kept my voice level, but could not resist making my point—that, as a salesman, it might be wise not to address someone by their first name and refer to himself with a title. I'm sure he had no idea what I was talking about, but I know I was rude. Who was more rude?

GENTLE READER:

Let's call it a tie. You both violated basic etiquette, and as a result, you both missed your objectives. Miss Manners will attempt to smother a feeling of smugness that rudeness was its own punishment.

Had the salesman addressed you respectfully, he presumably would have obtained a hearing. Had you made your point without the rudeness of reprimanding him—instead, saying civilly, "I am the person in authority, and I prefer to be addressed as Ms. Smith"—he might have understood.

DEAR MISS MANNERS:

I just received a phone call from the account representative at the bank where my husband and I have a joint checking account. The woman asked for my husband, and since he was not home, I asked to take a message. She told me it was personal, so I informed her that I am his wife and couldn't she tell me what the call was concerning.

She said no. So I asked her if the call was regarding bank business. (We have no other business with the bank.) She responded by telling me that she had called to discuss opening a savings account with my husband. At that, I said "Fine," and we hung up.

Now I feel bewildered. Why would she call to speak specifically with my husband and tell me it was personal? Am I out of line asking what "personal" could mean? Please help me know, because I don't know what to think!

GENTLE READER:

Rarely does Miss Manners have such a chance to relieve a person's mind by explaining the misuse of etiquette, as she will now do for you.

She supposes that you are imagining that the lady does, indeed, have personal business with your husband that she wants to conceal from you, and has used her identification with the bank as a cover.

Miss Manners doubts this to be the case. More common than private deceit nowadays is the false use of terms of friendship in order to do business. Consider how many strangers have addressed you by your first name in commercial transactions. The most likely explanation is that the caller was working mindlessly from a list of names and had been told to talk only to those people directly. By "personal," she meant that she wanted to talk to him "in person," so to speak.

Certainly that is the theory you should offer when reporting the incident to your husband. Should it happen again, you might want to consider changing banks. Or husbands.

With Whom Am I Speaking?

DEAR MISS MANNERS:

My name is Maria. I work as a sales representative selling products over the phone. My name is very common and I often encounter many other Marias.

How do I leave messages on other Marias' voicemail without sounding redundant? I always felt odd about saying, "Hello Maria, this is Maria." I always say, "Hello Maria, this is Maria Smith" (I give her my full name). Is this correct? How do I best address this?

GENTLE READER:

Centuries ago, this problem was almost as acute as it is now. People had only first names and, as most of these tended to be widely used, it was difficult to distinguish among individuals. The custom arose of attaching that person's father's name (Johnson) or occupation (Smith) or hometown (de la Ville) for the sake of clarity. In time, these became attached to families and became surnames.

Miss Manners congratulates you on having reinvented the idea. You already have a surname, and you have wisely decided to use it. This already lessens the Maria-this-is-Maria effect.

But history has even more help to offer. As there came to be alternative ways of addressing people, it was possible to make a distinction between one's intimates and, well, sales representatives and other non-intimates. So the correct way to address your customer is with an honorific and her surname: "Mrs. Johnson, this is Maria Smith."

Press One

DEAR MISS MANNERS:

Am I just an old grump, or do others find those telephone "menus" terribly rude?

I'm referring to those systems, so popular with businesses, that say, "If you want A, press 1; if you want B, press 2" and so on, ending with, "If you want to hear a human voice press # and get put on hold." The message, at least it seems to me, is, "We want your business (i.e., money) but we can't be bothered talking to you or treating you as a fellow human being."

Or maybe I am just out of touch with the times. After all, as I'm told, it's "for your convenience." Don't see it, though.

GENTLE READER:

If there is one phrase that never fails to set off the Old Grumps Club, it is "for your convenience." Miss Manners is amazed that anyone can stay in business who is naïve enough to believe it will inspire customer gratitude.

Nevertheless, a properly programmed voicemail system actually can be a convenience for the customer. It gets routine questions answered with some degree of certainty, and it eliminates the embarrassment if you have to ask again.

But that is assuming that it has someone available for questions that are not covered and that it doesn't have so many choices that you are punching away at your telephone until you forget why you called.

DEAR MISS MANNERS:

A friend who is a most genteel man revealed that in a frustrated moment, after being in an hour-long loop of voice recognition commands for—I use this term advisedly—"customer service" of a major airline, he shouted the most vulgar expression in the English language into the telephone. To his surprise, he was immediately connected with a supervisor who solved his problem instantly.

Last week, after a bout with a telephone answering service that did not recognize the words "help," "operator," "live body," and the like, I too looked around to be sure my children were out of hearing and shouted "f——" into the telephone. To my shock, this phrase worked with my health insurer. I later brought this up with my husband, who turned red and shamefacedly admitted that he, too, had used this method to get through to a different airline.

I feel the practice of American corporations programming the phrase "f—— you" into their lexicon of recognized words, and the fact that this brings the fastest results, is truly demeaning to our culture. Would you please use your bully pulpit to request a universal, clean phrase to replace the current magic words?

GENTLE READER:

How about "Customer service, please"?

No doubt this is programmed to produce a recorded laugh.

Miss Manners is not so naïve as to expect the argument of civility or human dignity to be effective in appealing to airlines, let alone health insurers. But she will ask them this: Which customer would you prefer to have aboard? The one who quietly goes to another airline when yours doesn't respond satisfactorily, or the one who turns vicious when encountering a delay?

Note to Gentle Readers: Please do not use the information contained in the question as a tip. Please?

After the Beep

DEAR MISS MANNERS:

I have noticed a questionable trend in regard to returning telephone calls. Whenever I make a call, often work-related, and am directed to leave a voicemail message, I do so. My messages are usually detailed but concise and courteous, with my contact information included.

It seems that recipients of calls can now no longer be troubled to even listen to their messages; rather, they simply redial my number, often not even knowing who has called. Many of these calls begin with "You called me? Who is this?"

I then must recap the message I have just left. Am I wrong to feel that this is a discourteous practice? Some of my younger friends seem to find it acceptable.

GENTLE READER:

That the telephone is passing out of common use leaves Miss Manners with mixed feelings. For much of its existence, it was accustomed to announcing itself shrilly, without regard to what it was interrupting.

Then along came answering machines, followed by voicemail and caller ID, all of which gave the recipients back control over the timing of accepting calls. But when cellular telephones became ubiquitous, there was a peculiar reversion to considering them an immediate summons, despite their ability to identify and take messages.

So perhaps it is just as well that the movement seems to be returning to the written word. Your young friends probably pay more attention to texting than to telephone messages. They should change those misleading recordings that invite you to leave messages there.

But while those are in place, Miss Manners agrees that it is inconsiderate to treat messages as you describe. You needn't run through your explanation again. Just say, "I left it all on your voicemail, so I won't keep you now by repeating it."

DEAR MISS MANNERS:

When I called my credit union, due to a question I had regarding my IRA, I left a message on the answering machine of the appropriate employee, giving my name, telephone number, and reason for calling.

The person I called was in the office that day, but away from her desk. A week later, I called again, because that person did not return my call. My second call, too, was ignored. On that occasion, another employee also told me the person I was trying to reach was temporarily away from her desk. So one week later I called for the third time and spoke to the person I had called twice before.

Should I have reminded her that I called twice previously, and also asked her why she did not return either of my two previous calls, or should I have said nothing about the two previous calls (which is in fact what I did)?

GENTLE READER:

When Miss Manners hears of someone's being "away from her desk," she pictures that person dashing back to the ringing telephone, and feels as if she should say, "Oh, do be careful, don't trip, I can wait a minute."

But not two weeks.

It is not rude to complain about rude service, provided you refrain from doing it rudely. In addition to being polite, however, you probably want to be effective. People who ignore your calls are not likely to be attentive to your complaints. You could certainly have said, "I've left two messages for you already," provided you promised Miss Manners not to go bonkers if the response is silence or a blunt "I wasn't here," or a bald "Okay."

The way to command the attention of someone like that is to keep going up the chain of command until you find someone who is, or pretends to be, shocked at the bad service. Those who ignore the reprimands of their superiors are not likely to remain long enough to be a nuisance to their customers.

Being Pressed

DEAR MISS MANNERS:

In this electronic age, most of us are using cell phones often, either for calls, texting, or both. I have had friends complain to me about taking too long to return messages when they have tried to contact me.

Although I do try to be responsive in a timely manner, I sometimes am in places where it would be rude to take the call. And if I am visiting with people at the time, I am not sure it would be polite to be sitting there texting away. But I would be curious to get your opinion on how soon one should return messages.

GENTLE READER:

What is the nature of your relationship to these people, that they feel that they have the authority to keep you on such a short tether? Miss Manners would have thought that even a boss or a lover who refused to admit your privilege of having a life would quickly inspire rebellion.

She is aware, however, that people with no such claims now believe that they should be able to command your attention at any time merely because it is technologically possible.

Another curious result is that many people no longer know how to prioritize electronic approaches, the way they once sorted their mail: invitations answered quickly, love letters sooner or later depending on one's emotions about the writer, chattiness when one has the time to chat, and so on. Instead, everything is classified as a potential emergency. (Emergencies were not formerly sent by letter, and Miss Manners doubts that so many of them arrive by other means.)

Your choice is between being polite and thereby disappointing rude people, or satisfying them by being rude to others.

Did I Call at a Bad Time?

DEAR MISS MANNERS:

The other day I walked into the bathroom of our public library and immediately heard a man's loud voice coming out of a bathroom stall. I realized that he was (I hope) talking on his cell phone while seated. Kind of conducting business while doing his business.

I was feeling uncomfortable that this guy was on his phone while I occupied the stall next to him. I heard everything he said and was trying to be quiet so as to not create noises that could have been heard on the other end of his phone call. Eventually I reached that moment when I needed to flush and was concerned that the noise might be overheard by his client and be embarrassing, so not wanting to be rude, I hesitated to flush.

I realize that this is ridiculous; I shouldn't be worrying about this poor guy. After all, I wasn't going to the bathroom in his office! He was officing in the bathroom! What do you think the etiquette should be about cell phones in public bathrooms, who has the responsibility of courtesy, and really what IS courtesy? I have seen guys at urinals on the phone, too. At first I thought they were talking to themselves! I am serious with this question!

GENTLE READER:

Miss Manners believes you. She confesses to a moment of doubt when you got to the part about hesitating to flush, when she thought you were going to complain about being forced to take on an unwelcome—not to mention impractical and unappetizing—obligation.

But when you admitted feeling ridiculous, it became credible to her that a polite person might indeed be jolted into office manners by office sounds before thinking the situation through. We polite people have really got to learn to get a stronger grip on ourselves.

It does not follow, however, that the other gentleman was discourteous. Recklessly indiscreet, yes, but it takes more than that to be rude—which raises the question of why so many people are able to succeed.

Unsavory as telephoning from the bathroom may be, it doesn't actually break an etiquette rule. This is not because cellular telephones aren't covered—on the contrary, they are threatening to become an etiquette category all by themselves. It is because talking is permitted in bathrooms, without regard to how far apart the parties to the conversation are. Although shouting is rude, you really don't want Miss Manners to put a ban of silence in public bathrooms.

So the only person who can claim to be offended here would be the one on the other end of the telephone, should he be brought to an unpleasant realization of the circumstances (from which you are not responsible for protecting him). Miss Manners understands that you were offended, but is afraid that this is neutralized by the rule requiring people to pretend that they do not overhear one another's conversations.

DEAR MISS MANNERS:

I am a busy hairstylist, and I run a tight ship, with clients seldom kept waiting. However I am frequently kept waiting by clients who feel that it is their God-given right to be on their cell phones during their whole appointment. They are too busy talking to even greet me.

I had one such, who walked in on the phone, talked DURING her color application, the entire processing time, her shampoo (I had to signal for her to change ears so I could properly rinse the color out), the conditioning, the final rinse, her bang trim. When I turned my blow dryer on, she snapped her fingers at me, and pointed in the most imperious manner possible.

I was so flummoxed by her rudeness that I meekly turned the dryer off. I am a person who is seldom at a loss for words, but this left me speechless. I also decided that I would no longer put up with this kind of behavior, so I wrote to her and "fired" her. I sent her check back as well and kept a copy of the letter, just in case.

I want the message to get out: Clients, do not be rude to your stylists, we are people too, and are highly sensitive, as most artistes are!!!! We love to visit with our clients, and become part of their lives, so please do not treat us as nonentities by spending the bulk of your appointment chatting on your cell phone. Please limit cell use for REAL emergencies ONLY.

GENTLE READER:

Miss Manners was with you, even through the part about being a sensitive artiste, which she believes to be an oxymoron. Conducting business with you must take priority over whatever else the client is doing to pass the time. It is rude for her to fail to greet you, to be unable to comply with directions, to keep you waiting and, most certainly, to snap fingers and point. If she was committing the common offense of talking too loudly, that, too, would be rude.

But when you declare that the opposite of being treated as a nonentity is to be part of your clients' lives, and you resent their visiting with others because you want them to visit with you, you and Miss Manners part company.

You perform a professional service. No matter how many people confide in their hairdressers, you cannot consider that politeness demands that clients do so. Miss Manners would imagine that others in your business would be relieved to be allowed to go about theirs.

CHAPTER 4

Is This Meeting Over?

It was always Miss Manners' understanding that a business meeting meant shooing the staff into the conference room to discuss work. So it came as something of a surprise to discover that a corporate world that is inordinately proud of its focus and seriousness of purpose has wandered off from that businesslike approach.

It is true that in the old smoke-filled boardrooms, it was not always easy to make out who was present. But Miss Manners had the impression that, give or take a consultant or major client, staff meetings were attended by people who actually worked there.

Now friends may be rounded up for sales pitches disguised as meetings disguised as parties; actual customers are enticed into product focus groups; and family members are invited to corporate retreats. The advance of technology brought in the outside experts to calm nerves and provide perpetual retraining to increase efficiency by constantly changing the appearance and function of the basic work tools—computers, copiers, and telephones. It was easier when the issue was limited to correcting the stonecutter's typographical errors.

Miss Manners has heard of meetings in which people-in-the-flesh sit around a conference table texting and videoconferencing one another. Or at least looking as if they are. Once, snoring was a good indication of who was not paying attention. Now the skill of looking alert while checking email or playing solitaire has become a job necessity.

But actual staff members need not be present. They can be teleconferenced, remote-viewed or telepresenced from home or another continent. So the conference room may no longer be needed, which is just as well, because it has been overbooked for birthday parties and showers.

Noticing an increasing number of meeting absentees, in body or in spirit, business philosophers decided to, as they say, "reinvent the product." Naturally, the first thought was to provide free food, and the second, to provide entertainment. Discussing everyone's feelings and playing sensitivity games is not Miss Manners' notion of entertainment, but it seems to appeal to many. As do the catered meals for high-level people and the coffee and doughnuts for everyone else.

All this has only added to the age-old problem of meetings: the nattering on. Everyone agrees that meetings are repetitive and boring, and yet everyone jumps at the chance to repeat and bore others.

So she has another suggestion that may appeal to rugged entrepreneurs: Limit the meeting time so strictly that the person chairing it can keep saying, "We're running out of time—please stick to the point" and require attendees to make any notes after the meeting, thus eliminating the necessity for them to bring their toys.

Is Anybody Listening?

DEAR MISS MANNERS:

Have standards changed for paying attention in meetings or during business presentations? When I'm speaking and everyone in the group is furiously typing, I can't tell whether people are taking notes to preserve my pearls of wisdom or working on their novels, tweeting my every word to the universe, or texting their boyfriends. Can you offer guidelines for business meetings in the digital age?

GENTLE READER:

Yes, but you may not care for Miss Manners' good-faith assumption that you are paying attention to the answer. Etiquette dictates that you appear to be present at meetings at which you are, in fact, present. This can be done with occasional eye contact, nodding agreement if appropriate, and the well-placed question. Miss Manners does not intend to check whether your infrequent typing is to record a reminder to act on something suggested by the meeting speaker or to accept a dinner date.

DEAR MISS MANNERS:

A visitor is making a presentation to you and several other colleagues in the office, letting his (usually it is a he) gaze drift from person to person. Then, in the midst of making a point, perhaps engrossed or distracted by this effort, he stops drifting and stares you fixedly straight in the eye. This may go on for 10 seconds before he comes to, and resumes drifting—often only to snag again on someone else.

What can the stared-at person do during this peculiar form of pseudo-intimate public contact? Nodding or smiling even slightly looks stupid to one's colleagues. Not reacting at all feels embarrassingly weird. Looking away could be taken as rude. I was once advised to focus on the tip of the stranger's nose, but that seems even ruder.

I doubt the staring-speakers realize they are doing this at all, but am at a loss to figure out what, if any, facial response they would be least put off by. Sometimes I've noticed a visible nod or eyebrow-raise puts them off their stride worst of all.

GENTLE READER:

You have your instructors, who come up with notions such as the tip-of-the-nose one that you have the good sense to reject, but those speakers have theirs.

Theirs are advising them to find a sympathetic listener and establish eye contact so that they seem actually to be talking to people, rather than past them. Signal back rejection, and they will probably go looking for another line of work, perhaps in mid-speech. Yet go into complicated animation, and they will forget what they are saying.

The kindest thing for the listener to do is to brighten the look in the eyes and to move the lips almost imperceptibly into a half smile. Miss Manners assures you that not even pseudo-intimacy is involved in the unspoken question ("Is anybody listening?") and a politely encouraging response.

Ten seconds is not long to suffer for an act of charity. And don't worry about your colleagues—they are either listening or daydreaming, but in any case, not watching you.

Calling to Order

DEAR MISS MANNERS:

I am the treasurer on a 6-person, all women, board in an 80-unit condominium complex. I attempt to treat everyone with respect and dignity and am dismayed that the majority of people do not return the same behavior. Only 5 positions are currently filled, with 2 experienced members and 3 new members (3 months since election) that form the majority. During meetings, the newest members interrupt those speaking, make accusations of bad behavior and wrongdoing without facts. They gang up on individuals, raise their voices, mimic and mock people, and tell those speaking to shut up. The person that tells people to shut up is a former nun and she says "stop" rather than using the actual words but that does not change her intent.

We have a property manager who should create a respectful atmosphere; however, she has joined the rabble-rousers. The manager is unhappy with the experienced board members because they want her replaced for many reasons that include not fulfilling her contract. The fact that the majority seem to feel their behavior is appropriate makes the two remaining board members powerless.

I am at a complete loss as to how to bring some sort of civility to meetings. Do you have or are you able to suggest a book that provides a guideline for proper behavior during small community meetings? I'm not speaking of something that provides rules such as *Robert's Rules of Order* but something that explains how to make a motion and the proper method of discussion. Explanations of addressing one another and anything that will aid in creating a respectful atmosphere would be helpful.

GENTLE READER:

Actually, Robert is exactly the person you should be checking with. Not only does he speak to the questions of how to make a motion, he has a section on how to deal with "disorderly words." And he speaks with an authority second only to Miss Manners' own.

DEAR MISS MANNERS:

How do you deal with a coworker who dominates meetings and is so self-absorbed?

GENTLE READER:

So self-absorbed that what? It is the job of the person who called the meeting—generally the boss—to manage it. If he is not doing so, you might ask him if his employees' time might not be better used than in long meetings.

DEAR MISS MANNERS:

I have attended several courses/workshops, some costly, and all scheduled for a limited time period, and I am made uncomfortable right from the start.

The first thing the course conductor does is to order the participants, one by one, to identify themselves and divulge personal information to the room full of (mostly) strangers. I don't want my privacy invaded and my safety compromised; I want the conductor to get right to the course material!

Nothing is stopping the course attendees from getting to know each other, on their own, if they have the inclination. I believe this time-wasting and nosy practice should be eliminated.

GENTLE READER:

This is one of those leftovers from the popular therapy craze of the second half of the twentieth century, when it was believed that people accomplish more when they become pals. It is in direct contradiction to what every schoolteacher knows about separating friends during class.

Miss Manners would have thought the custom would have been dropped by now. Surely we have all sat captive through enough long professional and personal résumés, in both the bragging and the whining modes, to know better.

When your turn comes, you can at least not add to the tedium. You need only state your name, your profession if it happens to be related to the subject matter of the course, and your level of ability in regard to the class. Having been regaled by others, your classmates are not likely to beg for more, but if they do, you should reply modestly that this is all that is relevant.

Calling In an Order

DEAR MISS MANNERS:

A colleague has offered to bring coffee to an upcoming meeting of about five people, and I'm wondering if it's appropriate to offer my coworkers particular coffee preferences. With everybody's unique coffee demands nowadays (half-caf, double whip, extra hot, with room) is it reasonable to offer these known preferences, or do I wait for the person offering to ask?

I'm pretty sure they want everybody to be happy with the coffee they bring, and I think the others would certainly appreciate that personalized touch—but I feel like I might be turning the kind offer to bring coffee into more than what was initially offered.

I realize it would be unreasonable to make these specialized requests for a group of 20. What would be your threshold for how big a group this would be acceptable?

GENTLE READER:

"May I get anyone some coffee?" is such a courteously collegial prelude to a meeting that Miss Manners hates to see it disappear.

But it is not going to survive if the generous colleague is pelted with orders for espresso, regular, cappuccino, mocha, Americano, frappuccino, caramel, or iced, and instructions in pseudo-Italian about the size and whether the milk should be steamed, foamed, or spillable.

This is not to say that people should not get the coffee they want, which they can easily do by bringing it in themselves. But a casual offer is different from designating someone to get the lunches, which involves writing down who wants a sesame seed bagel and make sure not to get poppy seeds, who wants only the kind of yogurt that has to be stirred, and so on.

Miss Manners would say that the number of special coffee requests should equal what a reasonable person—or the particular person making the offer—can remember without writing anything down.

DEAR MISS MANNERS:

As a female research scientist at a public institution, I was invited to speak to a small group of non-scientist professional and businesswomen about my work. Although giving speeches is not an official part of my job, I accepted in the spirit of public education.

At the appointed hour, I arrived to find the audience finishing dinner. I received the impression that speakers are considered "entertainment" by this group, and thus are not worthy company for dinner. This was clearly a dinner event. I was not excluded from the business part of the meeting, only the socializing.

As some effort in preparation was required on my part, and there was no compensation involved (although I received a letter opener as a parting gift), I felt insulted. Is this accepted practice in the real world? It was my first and only experience speaking outside academic circles.

GENTLE READER:

What business and profession are these people in, that they classify a scientist discussing her research with a clown who pops in to entertain them (and charges for it)?

They don't seem to understand business entertaining, either. The protocol for a speaker is not just to invite her to the meal after which she is to speak, but to realize that she is doing an additional favor to accept. It gives some of the people, usually the organization's officers, an extra, less formal, opportunity to ask her about her subject matter. They should also apologize if it is unavoidable for her to spend time sitting through their business meeting.

Miss Manners sees no point in your brooding over this ignorance, which is now past. But she would suggest that you check arrangements before accepting a situation you find unpleasant.

DEAR MISS MANNERS:

We are hosting a luncheon at our home for the initial board meeting of a new nonprofit organization. We want to know if it is appropriate to serve wine at the luncheon.

GENTLE READER:

As you have already agreed to meet over a meal in a private home—yours—the line that Miss Manners would have drawn separating the private from the professional has been crossed. Since you are unable to walk a straight line, it seems inhospitable to hold your guests to a higher standard.

DEAR MISS MANNERS:

Should we seek to avoid holding business meetings at fast-food restaurants?

GENTLE READER:

What were the other choices? The drive-through or the driving range? Perhaps you should consider scheduling meetings between meal-times, say, during the workday.

CHAPTER 5

Love Me, Love My Laundry

Everyone hates business dress codes. If not for those outrageous orders to surrender individuality to conformity, we would all be free to wear jeans, T-shirts, and running shoes to work. Miss Manners' first sympathy is not usually for the boss, but when it comes to having to deal with the effect that startling looks have on clients, colleagues, and customers, she makes an exception.

The right to wear one's own choice of clothes has been elevated to a basic human right, the right, as it is inevitably put, to "be oneself." Never mind that everyone is trying to be someone else. The doctor dresses like an unemployed teenager; the architect dresses like a gym teacher; and the receptionist dresses like a member of an older profession. Being oneself means dressing to be the person you would like to be.

One would think that a society obsessed by the need to "project an image" would be willing to let someone with more taste and sense do the costuming. Such is not the case.

According to the employees, Casual Friday is too little or too much. Jeans are inappropriate, or the only appropriate attire. Earrings for gentlemen and low-cut tops for ladies are fashionable or incongruous. Flipflops are sensible or smelly. Miniskirts are stylish or trashy. Underwear as outerwear is chic or lewd. The wary boss tries not to look—and prays that someone will get some work done.

Business attire serves two important purposes, both of them symbolic. First, it conveys seriousness of purpose. The businesswoman who shows too much cleavage can argue until she is blue in the face that gentlemen should not be looking, but no one is watching her face. A professional look—whatever that means these days—shows that you are there to work.

Second, business attire gives an impression—possibly an incorrect one—of competence. The surgeon who visits your bedside dressed for his golf game may be a miracle worker in the operating room, but does he make you feel better? One is more inclined to believe in the advice of a pharmacist who wears a lab coat than that of one who wears a cut-off T-shirt. This is not fair, but we make judgments on the clues we are given.

Strict uniformity is not the only alternative. Many components of dress have symbolic importance that have nothing to do with work. Headscarves, hats, jewelry, and hairstyles may be worn for reasons of religious conviction. The right question is whether the religious symbolism is consistent with the underlying premise of the professional symbolism, i.e., a commitment to the job.

The same standard should be applied to "personal touches," easier though those may be to navigate. The employee who demands the right to dress as he sees fit makes a choice. It is not unreasonable to expect that he make such choices with the same intelligence he is expected to display during the rest of his workday.

DEAR MISS MANNERS:

My boyfriend and I got into a big debate last night about business ethics. We disagreed on the fact that appropriate appearance, amongst other factors of course, is a part of conveying business in an ethical way.

My boyfriend felt that "appearance has absolutely nothing to do with ethics." I felt it did: showing up on a service call (as an electrician) in yesterday's "wife-beater," unshaven, was not the most ethical way of conducting business. I believe in looking sharp, because it conveys a certain level of competence and gives the client confidence in the serviceman and the services that they are about to receive.

My boyfriend felt that as long as you are doing a great job and not cutting corners, it doesn't matter, whatsoever, how you look—as long as you get the job done right. "It's part of staying true to myself—it's who I am," he felt. His arms and back are covered with major tattoos, and although beautiful, they can be intimidating to an elderly housewife or else tempting/sexually suggestive to a desperate one. (Ha!) Anyway, I am rooting for a clean shirt versus the "I just rolled out of bed and I am sexy" look.

GENTLE READER:

You are talking at cross purposes, because while you are right that appearance is extremely important, the gentleman is right that it is not a matter of ethics, in the way that doing an honest job is.

It is naïve to think that who he "is" does not change with the situation in which he finds himself. That he is a sexy guy who just rolled out of bed and may be ready to return to it may be thrilling to you. To a client yearning only to have her wiring fixed, it is probably the last signal she hopes to get from a stranger with whom she is expected to be alone in the house. And if it is not, Miss Manners suspects that the gentleman may be on the receiving end of some less subtle signals.

Compulsory Casual

DEAR MISS MANNERS:

What are the acceptable and practiced rules of business casual dress in the employment world? We are employed at a billing center for a national durable medical equipment supplier. Our manager has recently reinstituted the business casual dress code. We had been quite casual (jeans) for a very long time. Does business casual allow "crocs" and does it allow employees to be wrapped in blankets at their cubicles during the winter months?

GENTLE READER:

As far as Miss Manners can tell, the word "casual" has come to mean that all social decencies are optional.

People who refuse to consider others—such as not showing up when they said they would or helping themselves to other people's lunch supplies—will brag that they are just casual sorts of people. The implication is that anyone who objects is pompously citing an unimportant technicality.

So if you think winter was rough in your office (would turning up the heat have helped?), wait until summer.

While "business casual" was originally intended to eliminate ties and jackets, Miss Manners urges your manager to specify what he means and drop that word "casual" from his dress code memos. Otherwise, you can expect your colleagues to peel down amazingly when it gets hot out.

RE-DRESSING COLLEAGUES

DEAR MISS MANNERS:

I work for a financial services company. We are not on Wall Street and don't adhere to the strict dress codes you would expect there; in fact, we have a somewhat casual dress code.

Because I'm in a position where I regularly interact with the CEO (who almost always wears ties and often suits) and other executives, and because I could possibly be in front of the media on any given day, I tend to dress more formally than many people here. I love getting dressed up, enjoy wearing jewelry, and usually choose to wear dresses or suits.

On a day when I was wearing a suit jacket, my supervisor commented about my clothes, saying something like, "My, you're awfully dressed up today."

I found his comment to be odd, in part because I was taught not to comment on anyone's clothes unless you're giving a compliment. His comment also prompted me to pause and wonder if I'm dressing up too much and possibly making him uncomfortable. He generally wears what I would call fairly casual clothes, unless he has specific meetings that call for a necktie, etc.

Is it rude of me to dress up in a way that's often more formal than the clothes worn by my boss? Is it simply not the smartest thing to do?

GENTLE READER:

It amazes Miss Manners that there is, in general, less tolerance for everyday formality than for the lack of it. Gentlemen who show up properly dressed for any but the most casual of occasions are inevitably ordered to remove their ties and jackets.

There is indeed such a thing as overdressing, but that is when one ignores the conventions of the situation: the equivalent of ignoring the conventions by underdressing. As you have explained, you are dressed to do your job, which requires meeting with formally dressed executives and representing the company to the media. You could explain that to your supervisor, or you could simply say good-naturedly, "This IS my casual look; you should see my dressed-up look."

DEAR MISS MANNERS:

In our office environment, which is on a military installation, there is no dress code except for those who are serving in the armed forces.

But it has always been understood that most people would dress in a professional manner, especially when dealing with the public.

We have a lady who is expecting a baby and beginning to show. This lady dresses to be cool since the temperatures are so high lately. The problem is that she wears maternity shorts and a short T-shirt that exposes her belly.

Some people feel that she isn't appropriately dressed, and they are repulsed by having to look at her unborn baby being so exposed. Isn't that why there are specific shops available for women that are pregnant?

This is a very delicate matter. It's really hard to tell this woman that she is repulsive and should cover her body! How does one approach a subject tactfully and professionally without making the situation worse? At this time, she has a few more months to go until full term. I'm afraid of what she may wear in the near future. I'm embarrassed for the woman. I think her attitude is that if you don't like it, don't look!

GENTLE READER:

Does the summer military uniform in your office feature bare midriffs?

Miss Manners does not otherwise know how to account for your unseemly insistence that the issue is that people consider the lady's exposed belly repulsive because she is pregnant. Surely you don't want to get into an argument about the beauty of expectant motherhood, among other reasons because you would lose.

By comparison, it will be a simple matter to cite regulations about professional dress. These make some concessions to comfort but—last time Miss Manners checked the military uniform—do not allow bellies to hang out in the heat, regardless of whether they are filled with babies or beer. Neither should their civilian colleagues.

DEAR MISS MANNERS:

What is the most appropriate way to tell a female colleague that her thong is showing above the waistline of her pants when she is seated? I wouldn't hesitate to politely (and discreetly) tell a coworker if her slip were showing, but this just seems different.

GENTLE READER:

That is not the only thing that is different now. You can no longer count on ladies' being upset when they find out that their underwear is showing. Miss Manners suggests saying quietly and neutrally, "You seem to have some elastic or something showing," so as to warn those who may care and not appear to be chastising those who do not.

Re-Dressing the Boss

DEAR MISS MANNERS:

I am an engineer and my boss is an engineer. In fact, I'm the only female engineer in our group (about nine people) and to complicate matters, I'm single. That may or may not be relevant.

My boss occasionally wears what we used to call high-waters—pants that are way too short for him. I think they look downright silly but I think he's oblivious. To prove my point, when he interviewed me for this job, he had the worst, most incomplete shave I've ever seen on a grown man. I should point out that he's also unmarried and despite these little fashion complaints, I think he's a good guy.

So the problem is, do I tell him about the high-waters? I wouldn't want my comments to be misunderstood as either a come-on or overly motherly. The guys in the group just wouldn't understand—I doubt if they've noticed either! I would tell him if he had mustard on his nose. Is this the same thing?

GENTLE READER:

In a word, no. Mustard on the nose can be removed in a second. What you want to do on your boss is a general makeover.

Even if you were friends, this would be questionable. Taste is not a matter of absolutes (in the way that absolutely everyone, with the possible exception of the hot dog vendor, agrees that mustard does not belong on the nose), and what you find silly others might find fetching. Miss Manners will not insult you by noticing your interest in this gentleman's unmarried state, but she will mention in passing that personal criticism is no way to start a friendship.

What you now have is a professional relationship where undue interest in people's appearances is unseemly and, in some cases, illegal. Were the other engineers to offer you gratuitous advice on changing your makeup or suggest that your clothing should be closer-fitting, you would—or at least Miss Manners hopes you would—be outraged.

DEAR MISS MANNERS:

I'm a 52-year-old executive who recently joined an Internet startup as VP. My trouble is that the company founders, both age 26, have very poor manners. One brings his German shepherd to work and lets it run around the office freely. The other has, on several occasions, shown up to an important meeting with a client wearing socks but no shoes. Even worse, both habitually arrive to meetings and scheduled events late. Am I right to voice a complaint about this?

GENTLE READER:

Haven't you ever dreamed of having your very own company, so you could do exactly as you pleased, without anyone to get in your way? And was it part of that dream that you would pay an executive to cast a critical eye on you and issue complaints about the way you behaved?

No?

Personally, Miss Manners agrees with you that professional behavior is preferable to aping the style of adolescents at leisure. But it isn't her company, either.

What you can consider yourself hired to do is to improve business. So if you can cast this as a business problem, go ahead. It would have to be something about the company image misleading people into thinking it was a sloppy operation, or the handicap of negotiating with stuffy people when they start out mad because they have been kept waiting.

If not, Miss Manners recommends confining your instruction to setting an example of professionalism with your own dress and behavior.

PERSONAL TOUCHES

Here's an idea for a break in the tedium of the workplace: Dress-up Friday.

Once a week, just for the fun of it, and on the day when nobody is concentrating on work anyway, workers could dress up in the style of the job each purports to be doing.

Doctors and ice cream vendors would wear white coats. Teachers and poets would wear tweed jackets. Businesspeople and high-priced escorts would wear pinstriped suits, the latter with nipped-in waist-lines. Farmers, house painters, and artistic painters would wear overalls. Waiters, musicians, and people with opera tickets or dinner invitations would wear evening clothes.

Nobody who wasn't in the military would wear all or part of a military uniform. All the people wearing workout or sports clothes would be working out or playing sports. People who were lewdly dressed could safely be presumed to be in lewd lines of work.

Tourists and journalists would dress in the style of the places and occasions they wished to observe, whether or not they felt superior to the people involved.

Everybody attending a funeral would be dressed in black. Nobody attending a wedding would be dressed in black, other than gentlemen's formal clothing. Children would not dress as adults, and adults would not dress as children.

Furthermore—and here comes the zinger—underwear would be worn under outer clothing, rather than instead of it.

Miss Manners has something in mind with this proposal, other than being vilified for attacking our most basic freedom—our constitutional right to look like fools for the creative purpose of offending our fellow citizens. Without quarreling with the principle of choice in fashion, lest someone try to resurrect the whalebone corset (thus endangering whales and ladies alike), she would like a small respite from the current confusion.

There is the aesthetic confusion. Nothing matches. People engaged in the same activity seem to be costumed for a chaotic variety of different lives. Whereas people were once embarrassed if they had misunderstood the dress code of an occasion, they do it purposely now because they believe there shouldn't be any. Even couples emerge unmatched from the same home to attend the same event—more often now, the gentleman more formally dressed than the lady.

Then there is the symbolic confusion. Who's in charge here? Who's even employed here? And who is serious enough about the job to assume its identity during working hours, rather than fighting it? It would be useful to have these questions instantly answered, which is why the system of professional dress codes developed in the first place.

But Miss Manners realizes that this was before creative dressing became the national pastime. She is only suggesting it as a novelty, now that all the creative dressers are dressed for all occasions in the same jeans and khakis.

Undress

DEAR MISS MANNERS:

A few weeks after joining a social organization, I received an invitation to hear a speech by a diplomat, followed by a "formal" dinner to honor the speaker. No other indication of dress was sent with the invitation. However I was warned to arrive before 6 p.m., as no one would be admitted after that time.

I left my office at 5 p.m. and arrived, to be admitted, at 5:50 p.m. I did not have time to change my clothes and I wore my skirted business suit. The gentlemen were all wearing dinner jackets and the ladies formal gowns.

In the ladies' room one of the women suggested I should have taken a gown to work and changed before coming. Others nodded agreement.

I was under the impression that a lady's skirted business suit was always correct wear, even if the gentlemen were wearing dinner jackets. Am I wrong? Should I have followed the suggestion made by the other ladies? Or given the degree of difficulty and the time constraints involved, should I have just graciously declined the invitation? In spite of all of this, I did enjoy myself very much.

GENTLE READER:

Do you suppose that "formal" means that gentlemen must dress up, but ladies are excused from doing so on the grounds that they would naturally be coming straight from work?

You are mistaken, as you found out, but Miss Manners confesses to being delighted about this mistake. We have come a long way if a lady can assume that gentlemen have the time and inclination to gussy themselves up, but everyone understands that ladies have more important claims made upon them.

On the contrary; busy and powerful businesspeople keep evening clothes at their offices for quick changes. Miss Manners is glad you had a good time anyway, but in the future please do your hosts the courtesy of dressing in keeping with the occasion.

DEAR MISS MANNERS:

I am a product manager for a local manufacturing company, where I have worked 11 years. For a customer/employee party, I wore a sweater with black sequins and matching black slacks. In my opinion and my boss's opinion, I looked great. But the boss's wife said that slacks were inappropriate. I need your opinion.

GENTLE READER:

Slacks may or may not have been inappropriate at this particular party—and black slacks with a dressy top are hardly outrageous these days, assuming that they are not being worn by debutantes and brides—but there was a lot that was.

It is inappropriate of your boss to tell you that you looked great, and still less appropriate of him to pass on his wife's criticism (unless that lady gave it directly, which would also be inappropriate). Is there any such thing as professionalism in your company?

Undressed

DEAR MISS MANNERS:

I am a female operating room nurse, and because of my work, I am required to change into scrubs every morning at the beginning of the shift and back to my regular clothes at the end of the shift. This takes place in a locker room with about 20 other female nurses present on any given day. Dressing and undressing in the vicinity of the other women has not bothered me until lately.

Some nurses seem to take this dressing room scenario as a "look-out" or rather a "check-out." I am a 46-year-old rather attractive female with a fairly nice body. Yet I have heard comments like "You should really think of breast implants" or "Have you put on some weight lately?" or "Gosh, what big feet you have" (#9 shoes). Frankly, this has left me speechless.

Is there any polite way to shut these people up? I do not want to insult them, but I do not want to hear these kinds of comments either. I am also curious if comments like these are an American custom. I was raised in Northern Europe, where these kinds of comments have never been acceptable.

GENTLE READER:

Do you mean "custom" as in "Sure, go ahead and criticize other people's bodies, it shows you really care" or as in "Why do so many people think they can do this?"

Miss Manners assures you that personal insults are not acceptable anywhere in the world, although they sure are common around here. Fortunately, politeness does not require you to accept them, as long as you don't snap back "You're no oil painting yourself."

She suggests saying something like, "I'm just changing clothes; I didn't sign up for the figure clinic." If that doesn't work, you may change your tone from lukewarm to cold and say, "I really don't care to hear this."

Ring Ring

DEAR MISS MANNERS:

I need advice about nose rings. I am very willing to have people decorate themselves however they wish, but this has an unusual wrinkle. I am a physician in a large community hospital that has an arrangement with a university hospital whereby their resident physicians (doctors in training) spend many months at our facility for education and experience. Of course, this requires them to care for our patients along with us.

While my patients and I have come to expect casual attire and earrings (regardless of gender), a recent young man has presented our first nose ring. He is bright and capable, but this strikes many patients and some staff as less than the professional image that our hospital strives to project. I should add that he does not appear to belong to an ethnic or religious group that is associated with body jewelry. His university has not done anything, and so far, neither have we.

Are nose rings now accepted professional attire? If not, should this be discussed with him and if so, by whom?

GENTLE READER:

No, nose rings are not professional attire among physicians, or Miss Manners would insist that you have one installed. Unlike you, she is not willing to allow people to decorate themselves however they wish and pretend that their choices have no symbolic effect on others.

In this case, the nose ring—and by the way, that "casual attire"—affects the patients. They don't say anything because they don't have the authority and anyway, they don't feel up to arguing. But Miss Manners assures you that the very idea of being treated by someone who is casual about his profession scares the daylights out of them.

Teaching professionalism is part of what your hospital is supposed to be doing. Miss Manners suggests that you and other staff members include training on how to project professionalism symbolically.

DEAR MISS MANNERS:

Is a gold ring with the company logo only appropriately worn during work hours? Right hand only if no wedding band, left hand, or either hand?

GENTLE READER:

There is nothing incorrect about wearing the company's ring after hours, on either hand. But before you decide to wear it on your wedding ring finger, with or without a wedding band, Miss Manners begs you to consider the symbolism. Whom would you prefer to thrill—your boss or your actual or potential spouse?

CHAPTER 6

The Eeeew Factor

The two big lies of the modern workplace—that the old hierarchies are gone, so that all employees are equal, and that these new "teams" are as bound together by friendship as by the accident of employment—have tangibly transformed offices. Walls and doors kept disappearing as the open office plan, divided only by small, flimsy, and moveable partitions, took over. Miss Manners loves the rhetoric that the designers and enthusiasts supply with it—about how nobody needs status symbols, everyone is working together, and there is no place any more for intrigue and plotting.

She is less crazy about what she hears from the workers. Being thrown closer together with their colleagues does not inspire them to equal rapture. From the complaints she gets, they can barely eke out tolerance for those with whom they are in such collegial proximity.

For starters, everybody smells bad. Or so everyone else reports to Miss Manners, although the complaint is evenly divided between those who smell bad because they don't use commercial products and those who smell bad from using commercial products.

In addition, everybody's coworkers scratch, belch, cough, spit, and produce what one Gentle Reader gently referred to as "noxious emissions." And that's only their normal state. They also come in sick and spread germs, or stay out well, taking sick leave and making others do their work.

They dress too sloppily or too provocatively. They keep running outside to smoke or they stay and keep popping their chewing gum. They bring things to eat and then refuse to share them. Or they bring treats for others and are annoyed that others never bring treats for them.

Although everyone agrees that sharing information and cementing relationships is the purpose of the open office plan, some of the people who work there are intrusively chummy and the others are unpleasantly standoffish. They are talking constantly, or they are constantly eavesdropping. They snoop by reading the papers on people's desks and the monitors of their computers. They talk on the telephone so loudly that people who don't want to snoop can't help overhearing.

Quick, where is the office carpenter? Let's wall in all these awful people so the sweet-smelling ones can get their work done in peace.

There are less drastic solutions available, but Miss Manners is afraid that these depend on restraint and good will, both of which seem to be in short supply. The offended person has to be willing to make a complaint in a way that avoids embarrassing the offender, and the offender has to be just embarrassed enough, anyway, to decide to change.

Traditional methods of doing this are to channel the complaint through a personal friend or to generalize it so that the guilty party knows who the object of it is but is allowed to think that nobody else does. A stronger version is to have the boss pass on the information with an air of not having noticed any offense, personally, but of merely reporting what more finicky people are saying. This is known as a warning.

You remember what good it did when attention was drawn to widespread offenses caused by smoking and flirting.

If the offenders don't care whether they offend—except to take pleasure in doing so—etiquette, which depends on voluntary compliance, is defeated. To answer that taunt of "Who's going to make me?" it calls in its tough older brother, the law. A working environment in which bathing, dress codes, and gossiping are regulated by law would be a mite totalitarian even for Miss Manners, but we could get there.

Cooperation is needed to stave it off, but professional distance would also help. Miss Manners doesn't just mean geographical distance, which is not always possible, but the distance of a demeanor that is almost the opposite of the current friendship model of workers' behavior, but works better. This is the notion that people are there not because they necessarily like one another, but because they want to get the job done in the most pleasant and efficient way possible.

Smelly

DEAR MISS MANNERS:

As a veterinarian, I am accustomed to my patients coming into the office with an odor. I feel that it is part of my job to help clients deal with their pets' unpleasant odors.

I am, however, at a quandary as to how to deal with the humans who present with intolerable odors. Usually these clients do not have the excuse of having come straight from a hard day at manual labor, but rather just don't know that they have a marked body odor. It is so bad that I can't stand to be in the same room with them, and the other clients in the waiting room suffer as well.

I am wondering if and how I can inform these clients of their intolerable odor without offending them. I wonder how professionals in other fields deal with this problem.

GENTLE READER:

They are all wishing they had it as easy as you. No other profession has such a tactful opening into the subject.

Miss Manners recommends sniffing the pet, asking worriedly, "Has he just been out chasing cars?" and then laughing and saying, "Sorry, it's not him; you must have just come from the gym."

DEAR MISS MANNERS:

My boss just passed gas two times while in my work area. Both times he excused himself. We were both studying work on my computer screen, so I chose to continue speaking and pointing out features of the spreadsheet that we were discussing. I didn't acknowledge the interruption, his slightly embarrassed surprise, or the genuinely offered "excuse me."

Did I handle that the right way? I basically pretended as though it did not happen.

GENTLE READER:

Call it cowardly, but etiquette does indeed deal with the unspeakable by not speaking of it. Even your unfortunate boss needn't have mentioned it, provided he did not pull that trick of staring so as to pretend that someone else did it (perhaps because that would not have worked, as you were the only one there).

Your ignoring the incident was fine, but Miss Manners advises you to ask him, at another time, for an office with a window.

DEAR MISS MANNERS:

I share a small windowless office with another woman who has recently started wearing very large amounts of very strong perfume. I have noticed that I am getting headaches and that my nose has a burning sensation while she is in the office. When she leaves, the symptoms lessen but do not go away completely until I am out of the building. It is also so strong that when I take a break and walk outside, the smell of the fresh air is even altered!

Ordinarily you would think that I could simply say that I have noticed that there must be something about your perfume that causes me to have . . . and that she would feel sorry to have caused me discomfort and be glad to know and stop wearing it. However, my officemate has no regard for others and no matter how I approach her she will claim that I was rude to her and will make my life in this office worse than it is. Another problem is that she and I do a job that demands that we share information and work closely in a very demanding and time-sensitive job. She has at other times withheld information from me when she was irritated at me before. I could call on my boss, but would prefer to handle this on my own. FYI I am a nurse as is she, who should know better anyway than to wear such strong fragrance to work even though we do not have direct contact with patients.

GENTLE READER:

If her behavior is that bad, Miss Manners is grateful that a nurse with no regard for others has not been assigned to a patient ward.

Your purpose here is not to express your anger over the past, but to persuade her to alter her behavior in the future. Miss Manners suggests beginning with "Mmmmm, new perfume!" Next comes how sorry you are to be having a bad reaction, which you suppose is why hospitals often ban perfumes. Or maybe it's because some, like hers, are too good to waste at work.

If the response is explosive, you will have to appeal to a higher authority. But isn't this exactly the sort of situation that bosses are paid to deal with?

DEAR MISS MANNERS:

I like the coworker who sits next to me, but I hate it when she snacks at her desk. The other day she had some sort of smelly, lemony fish dish for lunch and I had to open the window. The smells are distracting and obnoxious. I would feel bad asking her not to eat at her desk, particularly since so many people in our company do. However, she is driving me crazy.

GENTLE READER:

You are fortunate to have a convenient window, and therefore a convenient solution. Well, two, but Miss Manners trusts that lemony fish is preferable to defenestration.

In case of smells, open the window as you did. If questioned, explain that the food smells so good it is distracting you from your work. The window will make the case more forcefully than you can in the heat of summer and the dead of winter.

Pushy

DEAR MISS MANNERS:

I work in an office of 30 people, and we have cake every month for birthdays, we have cake for weddings, we have cake for retirements, we have people who bring in cake on Fridays just to celebrate its being a Friday.

I always participate in the festivities by signing cards and wishing the person well, etc., but I usually don't care to eat the cake. Not because I dislike cake. Personally, I love cake. But if I ate all that cake, I'd be a blimp. I eat enough sweets at home as it is.

No one in my office is seriously overweight and it wouldn't bother me if they were, but for some reason people insist I eat cake, and when I decline, they take it personally. At least three people ask "Do you want cake?" or "Did you get cake?" or "Get some cake!" before I make it back to my office.

When I say no thanks, I get a sneer. Is there a nicer way to handle it, or should I just not worry, and if my not eating cake bothers them so much, so be it. This is a very small problem in the grand scheme of things.

GENTLE READER:

But it's a field day for Miss Manners. Have some cake.

No, wait. She doesn't mean that.

Oddly enough, neither do your colleagues. Their exhortations are really only blather intending to convey geniality. It's a pitiful sort of geniality that turns so easily to a sneer, but that is what they intend.

Social life is full of people who believe that attempting to force ever more food and drink into their protesting guests is an act of hospitality. The twist that particularly interests Miss Manners is that you are at work—if, indeed, anybody in that office has time to work between parties. Any socializing at work, beyond merely being pleasant and cooperative, is supposed to be voluntary.

To engage workers in constant compulsory partying, and then attempt to make the party food compulsory as well, is not just rude, it is a very odd definition of fun. Only when there is a blatant sneer will Miss Manners allow you to supplement your repeated "No, thank you" with a sweet, "Why, I thought I'd leave more for you."

Messy

DEAR MISS MANNERS:

I have been confronted with the problem of very dirty, unsanitary, even smelly shared food areas at work. I've never had a problem throwing stuff out—including dirty dishes because I feel that I'm helping to restore some cleanliness.

I'll do the dishes sometimes. I'm a guy, and don't feel I'm being taken advantage of too extremely if I do someone else's dishes now and then, but I have a female friend who feels that she is being unfairly taken advantage of if she cleans out a smelly refrigerator at work—the slobby guys are willing to put up with the smell and let the women clean it out. So she lets it rot and smell even though it's close to her desk. What would be the best way to handle unclean situations at work where slobs let things get unsanitary, and are willing to wait until somebody else takes care of it?

GENTLE READER:

Are you throwing out the dishes on those "sometimes" when you don't do them? Just asking. If so, no wonder your friend is washing her hands of the situation, so to speak.

DEAR MISS MANNERS:

When I go into the kitchen at work, I often find the microwave idle but containing someone else's lunch. People tend to forget about their lunches, or are unavoidably detained, and do not return for quite some time.

I am in the habit of just removing the container and setting it aside so that I may use the microwave for myself. I am careful not to stick my fingers in the food or spill anything. On one occasion, I overheard a coworker tell another, "Hey, somebody moved your lunch!" I didn't say anything, seeing nothing wrong with what I had done.

Who is at fault here, the person who selfishly monopolizes the microwave during the lunch hour, or the person who selfishly shoves the offending entree aside?

GENTLE READER:

Ah, the great laundry room problem, moved to the office kitchen. Miss Manners is grateful that you didn't dump the offending meal on the floor, as apartment dwellers sometimes do with their neighbors' underwear, in order to use the machines.

Never mind fault, as there needn't be any here. And the remedy, of the food's owner reheating it when he returns, is right there.

Grabby

DEAR MISS MANNERS:

One day I put a candy jar on my desk, and my coworkers changed from pleasant and polite human beings into rude, inconsiderate boors.

At first, they just came into my office with any bogus excuse, interrupting my work, phone calls, even conversations with the boss, to ask permission to take a piece of candy.

Later, they kept coming, but stopped asking. Instead, they started making tactless comments, such as, "Don't you have any GOOD candy?" and "What happened to all the caramels?" and "Who ate all the red jelly beans?" Some were accusatory, saying, "You're trying to spoil me" (or my diet or my teeth).

One coworker saw me replenish the jar, and went directly into my desk drawer to select the type of candy he wanted. Another brought her coffee cup to my office and emptied my jar into it, explaining that she didn't have time or money to go to lunch. Another would eat only certain colors or flavors, leaving only the black and white gumdrops or the orange and green jelly beans—and no one else would eat the picked-over ones, so they were wasted. One person actually tasted and spat out—in front of me—several pieces from a rather expensive box of chocolates until she finally got one she liked.

Needless to say, none of these people ever brought in a box or bag of candy to refill the jar—and keeping it stocked was running into money. I solved my problem by "running out" of the "good stuff" and keeping only hard candies of the least expensive kind in the jar.

But the question remains: Why did these people act in such an unmannerly fashion? I am sure they would not have behaved this way in a purely social setting (i.e., at a party). Yet when confronted with a display of hospitality at work, they forgot their manners altogether. I don't understand it at all, Miss Manners.

GENTLE READER:

Miss Manners does understand it, but wishes she didn't. It is not a nice clue to human nature. The speed with which people can change a courtesy into an entitlement is awe-inspiring.

She cannot even share your confidence that these people would not have acted this way at a party. The respect and gratitude that hospitality should inspire no longer inhibits people from managing the apparently contradictory impulses of complaining about what is available and grabbing all they can.

Your gradual withdrawal of hospitality was tactfully managed, and Miss Manners regrets having to agree that there is no point in offering such a purely luxurious kindness to ingrates. But she hates to stifle your generous impulses with such cynicism. An occasional offer of something you keep otherwise out of reach would perhaps alert the beneficiary to the fact that the treat did not merely grow wild on your desk, but was being voluntarily offered by an actual human being.

DEAR MISS MANNERS:

I work at a doctor's office where patients and others show their appreciation, especially at Christmas, with gifts, usually foodstuffs. These items are addressed to "staff" or "Staff and Dr." or simply handed to one of us.

Usually, the doctor or his wife, the office administrator, take these gifts home for their personal use without ever acknowledging that they were for the employees. One patient brought four boxes of candy, specifying two were for the physician and two for the rest of the office. None of us were offered even a sample! Another time, a container of candy handed to one of the technicians for the technicians was picked up by the doctor and placed on his private desk!

The entire staff finds this behavior offensive, but we are at a loss as to how to respond when gift-givers inquire how we liked their presents! What can we do?

GENTLE READER:

Tell the doctor and his wife that the staff must, of course, write a thank-you letter to the kind donors of these presents, but that you are all disturbed about being unable to describe the chocolates because you never tasted them. Therefore (you will continue) everybody has decided to thank the patients for their thoughts, and assure them that they will be hearing from those who actually got to enjoy the treat.

Please note that Miss Manners has phrased this threat in the plural. This is essential, so that no one person gets into trouble with the boss, but that he understands that he has an office-wide problem on his hands.

DEAR MISS MANNERS:

I work for a small law firm consisting of four attorneys, one of whom likes to share people's lunches. Sometimes he will take something out of the fridge; other times, he will take a little "nibble" while the person is eating lunch from their desk. Sometimes he is courteous enough to ask first; other times he will simply help himself if the person has walked away for a moment. Quite often, I eat lunch in my office and he will frequently ask me if I brought enough for two or if I need "help."

I'm on a diet, so I am very meticulous about counting calories, and I rarely bring extra food. I'm afraid that I'm just not as used to his behavior as everyone else in the office seems to be.

Once, his secretary asked me to guard her lunch while she stepped away for a moment. Despite my efforts, he did come by and eat all the chicken off of her chef salad.

After he ate my lunch a week ago, I started labeling my food. This made me feel like I was five. Worst of all, he tries to justify his behavior by saying that if someone leaves their lunch in the fridge for too long, it is "fair game." (I'm talking about a canned item that had been in the fridge for two days.)

I'm really not a stingy person, but I don't feel that I should have to share my lunch with an attorney who is more than successful enough to provide for himself. Should I just stop bringing food to work and eat out? Should I avoid eating lunch at my desk so that I won't have to fend him off? Would it be tacky to invest in a lunch box with a lock?

GENTLE READER:

He likes "to share" other people's property without their permission, especially when they aren't guarding it? And he deems it "fair game" to appropriate anything that is, in his opinion, left around "too long"?

Are these the terms your firm uses to defend clients who like to share other people's money that they leave lying around in the bank for too long?

Miss Manners is afraid that what you have there is a thief, although it would be kinder to state this in terms of psychological illness. Whether you condemn him for helping himself or take the position that he needs help, your lunch will disappear unless you protect it. And you and your colleagues need to keep up your strength so that you can deal with the worse trouble this person is bound to get into.

Wee Wee

DEAR MISS MANNERS:

There's a fellow at my end of the corridor at work who uses the ladies' room instead of the men's. There are few offices in our area, so I suppose he thinks it won't matter, and it does save him six or seven steps.

I'd like to get him to stop, but I don't want to embarrass him. I don't know him well enough to pull him aside and talk to him about it. I thought of posting a message on email, saying that I don't know who's doing this but to please stop. But I don't know how to phrase the message, and every option I think of seems like it'll embarrass either him or me or both.

GENTLE READER:

Miss Manners appreciates your reluctance to embarrass a fellow worker. That is kind. But surely this particular one does not have a very highly developed sense of embarrassment.

So let us see if we can develop it a bit, while respecting your polite unwillingness to cause him public embarrassment. We'll stick to private embarrassment. Here's your email message: "Warning! A man has been seen entering the ladies' room at the end of the corridor. His identity is unknown. If you should spot him, do not attempt to confront him. Lock him in the ladies' room from the outside, and alert Security immediately."

DEAR MISS MANNERS:

In our office, there are nine women and four men. The men's and women's rooms are identical, except for the labels on the doors. Occasionally when the women's room is occupied, I use the men's room as an alternate, rather than hang around in the hall wasting time.

Should I put the seat back up after I use it? We women always complain in our homes if our men leave the seat up, but, since this is technically their territory, I'd like to know what you think about this. I don't want any opinion on my use of the facility, only on the condition in which I leave it.

GENTLE READER:

Well, good. If you had, Miss Manners was considering putting it in the see-if-this-solves-itself file, as state laws are now beginning to mandate more restroom facilities for ladies than for gentlemen.

Miss Manners, in turn, does not want to supply anatomical reasons for her reply. The answer is that the completely closed toilet is the neutral position, which is how you should leave it.

HYGIENE AND HEALTH

The following dialogue is a faultlessly polite one, especially when you consider how awful one of the participants feels:

"You look terrible. Why don't you go home?"

"I feel terrible. But I'd feel just as bad at home, so I might as well get something done."

"Don't worry about the work, we'll manage."

"No, that's okay. I'm not going to leave you with all this."

The virtues that shine through this mannerly exchange are compassion, dedication, and self-sacrifice. One person only wants to relieve the suffering of another; the sufferer only wants to do his or her duty, without allowing the misfortune of illness to inconvenience others.

So Miss Manners feels terrible (but not terrible enough to stop working) about the fact that it ill serves the goal of pleasant living to which etiquette is dedicated. The person with the cold—one doesn't hear these protests from those who have appendicitis—remains unhappy, and not only because of the discomfort of the sickness.

The other person's sympathetic urgings deprive the ill one of the blessing of complaint. And about the only thing that makes one feel better in this state, aside from a good rum toddy, is moaning, in the hope of extracting further sympathy from those who have the effrontery to look fine.

Yet to continue to complain after having been told to leave work is dangerous. It brings on increasingly irritated retorts, from "Oh, stop being a martyr and get out of here," to "You're not much use, anyway." And it soon wipes out the good will that one could ordinarily expect to achieve from working when there is an obvious excuse not to.

The person without the cold is rendered even more unhappy by the exchange. To the irritation of having one's advice ignored are added the danger of catching the cold and the disgust of watching its physical manifestations. Those who purposely visit the sick feel wrapped in the immunity of virtue; those who have the sick visit them have no such protection.

If Miss Manners were in a line of work that seeks to relieve suffering any other way, she would strongly advise sick people to convalesce where they don't endanger or annoy others. But it is her task to relieve etiquette suffering, even when it arises from well-mannered imprudence.

Those who do stay at their offices while sick are obliged to follow etiquette rules that would be considerably relaxed if they took their misery home to their families. Among loved ones, it is occasionally allowable to exaggerate the discomfort of a minor illness in order to produce a response of soothing voices and comforting touches. (This only works if one does it rarely, one reciprocates, and if the victim maintains a tone of docility and gratitude. Loved ones have limits to their tolerance, too. Scorn the chicken soup, snap back at the "'There, there,'' and you will soon find yourself no longer within call of a friendly voice.)

At work, there is no excuse of being unable to help the manifestations of illness. All but the most delicate coughs and sneezes must be hidden from others. The grosser forms of cleaning up must be performed in a bathroom. Don't even think about applying nose drops where anyone else can see. Even the paraphernalia of illness—the discarded tissues, the bottles of drops—must be whisked out of sight. Only by pretending not to be all that ill, and making it convincing, can one expect to be tolerated at the workplace.

Notice that this rules out the relief of whining and complaining. A brave "No, really, I'm fine" may just possibly produce the admiration one feels due when refusing to succumb to illness, but Miss Manners suggests not counting on it.

Balms and Blessings

DEAR MISS MANNERS:

I work in an office where a nearby coworker yells "God bless you" whenever anyone sneezes within hearing distance, which is quite frequently. She even does this when she doesn't know who sneezes. I find it disruptive to my work, which involves dealing with the public on the phone—and I'm sure callers can hear it in the background.

I was taught to stifle sneezes and try to make them as unnoticeable as possible, so I would not disturb anyone or call attention to myself. Others were taught to acknowledge sneezes in their vicinity with a "God bless you" or "Gesundheit."

Which is the proper response? I once told someone I didn't comment on sneezes because I'm not superstitious, and he said, "I thought that was just being polite." Also, what should I say when I sneeze quietly and someone says "God bless you"—should I ignore it (with the hope that that person will follow suit in the future) or say "Thank you"?

GENTLE READER:

Everybody who has ever sneezed knows what it is to hold opposite ideas simultaneously—you want to head off the sneeze, but you really want to go through with it, as well. That's how it is with sneezing etiquette. Contradictions everywhere.

You are right that one should muffle one's sneezing, preferably in a nice, clean handkerchief, to make it as little noticed as possible; and the others are right that it is conventional to offer a blessing that proves that it was noticed.

You are right that the blessing arises from superstition (that the soul is being expelled), and so is the person who says that blessing is polite.

The only rudenesses Miss Manners can identify here would be failing to reply "Thank you" to the blessing, and yelling. The polite plea that your coworker is startling your callers and should administer blessings more in the tone traditionally associated with blessings would be more to the point than resisting this little convention.

DEAR MISS MANNERS:

I work in a very professional environment, so it caught me completely off guard today when a new coworker asked if I had a stick of lip balm. I replied, "Yes, why do you ask?" thinking that would give the hint.

But she inquired further, "Can I use it?" in front of a fellow coworker. I wasn't sure if I should have declined and risked insulting her hygiene by not sharing or instead obliged and looked too unconcerned about my own by lending it.

I opted to share. Did I do the right thing?

This new coworker also has some other habits that reflect poorly on her level of professionalism such as picking at her fingernails while someone is trying to explain something to her, cutting her cuticles while sitting in a meeting with someone in their cube, etc. Should I pull her aside privately to let her know this is not appropriate at work? (She is right out of school and this is her first professional job.) Or is this her manager's job (who is already aware of such behavior)?

GENTLE READER:

Now that you and your colleague are on the same stick of lip balm, Miss Manners has a hard time saying that you are not on sufficiently intimate terms to attempt to reform her. Nevertheless, you should let the manager do it and concentrate on protecting yourself from unreasonable demands and flying cuticles.

A vague "Sorry" at the start would have covered whether you actually possessed lip balm or were simply declining to share; as you discovered, bringing on the second question was not a good idea. If you are caught trying to explain work matters to this lady while she is busy grooming herself, the polite thing to do would be to offer to postpone work until she has completed her toilette.

DEAR MISS MANNERS:

What is the proper wording to announce to employees that someone in our office has a serious illness?

GENTLE READER:

Shouldn't you be asking the ill person, or, if that's not possible, the family?

That an employee's medical history is protected by law is not the only reason to refrain from setting off a chain of events that moves quickly from circulating a get-well card to speculating about who will get the job. This will happen anyway, Miss Manners is afraid, but the employer should state only what might affect the work schedule ("Violet Valéry will be on extended medical leave") adding only whatever else the employee has authorized, such as the nature of the illness and the prognosis.

To the chorus of "What happened?" a discreet response would be something like, "Concerned friends can contact her partner at the home number."

CHAPTER 7

The Attention Deficit

The doorbell is buzzing. The land telephone is ringing. The computer is beeping. The cellular telephone is vibrating. The printer is flashing. The fax is making that thumping sound. The kettle is screeching.

And that's just for the person who works quietly at home, with no one around to bother her (or to tend to the crying baby).

What is the correct order in which to attend to these summonses? The doorbell is announcing a package that is unlikely to reappear, as the deliverer failed to put its number on the We Tried note. Caller ID says that a client is on the line, no doubt wanting to know when the project will be finished, and the computer is beeping because there is a message from the supervisor, wanting to know when the project will be finished. The cellular telephone is vibrating with a call from that dear friend who begged to have her child picked up at day care because "I have to stay late, and you have nothing to do." The printer is demanding more paper, while the fax machine is turning out lewd advertisements. The kettle is ready for tea.

Miss Manners would go first for the tea, to calm her enough to comfort the baby. Ah, for the quiet of an office, where there are no doorbells and, with any luck, no babies.

But there are grown people there, who are just as insistent. And in the modern open office, the cubicle offers no protection. Even those high-ranking enough to have actual doors feel obliged to announce an open-door policy lest they seem insensitive to employee concerns.

Turning away any interruption seems rude to those who go by the social rules, in which a live person trumps electronic or other intrusions. Miss Manners knows this will come as a shock to those who concentrate on team spirit to the exclusion of the goal, but at work socializing should be a marginal activity.

Although in the business world, it is rank that matters, the work itself sometimes matters even more. The wise boss does not interrupt a customer sales representative who is waiting on a customer for anything that does not require evacuating the building.

Yet bosses, coworkers, outsiders, and their electronic summonses do not seem to be aware that quality work demands paying attention. "Can't you see I'm trying to work?" is a concept that is taken as an admission of failure at what is now known as multitasking. It is enough to make everyone at the office long to trade the microwave for the kettle and telecommute.

DEAR MISS MANNERS:

My place of employment is populated by very nice people, but a few seem to have a lot of spare time, which they spend visiting up and down the hall. Usually I just tell them if I don't have time, but one of these gets on my last nerve.

He seems to sense when a topic is slightly aggravating to me and comes by at least twice each day, sticks his head into my office, and brings up that subject, relentlessly carrying on until I tell him to drop it, which he does—until the next visit. There have been occasions when I felt myself about to lose control and shriek at him. For example:

Him: "Well, bought that car yet?"

Me: "Nope. Still looking. May not buy one for months."

Him: "You know, your car may not hold up that long! You'd better go out tonight and look!"

Me: "No, I've been looking and it's going along about as well as can be."

Him: "You are going to need a reliable car for the field trip to Oshkosh. Get out there and look."

Me: "Okay, enough already."

If I eventually do buy my car, within a day or two I'll hear "Hey, signed up for that course with the office computer expert yet?" or "So, going to paint your house this year?"

In his case, if I said, "I can't talk now, got to work," I'd be saying it every time he appeared at my door. I have tried to just continue doing my work, giving him only half my attention, but he is also incredibly persistent.

I have known this person for years, and absolutely guarantee that he's not romantic or trying to capture my fancy. Further, he is intelligent and well-traveled. I don't really want to make an enemy of him, yet that's exactly what's going to happen if I blow up some day. It's mostly the extreme irritation I feel at my concentration being broken for such a stupid conversation that frazzles me.

GENTLE READER:

As giving him half your attention doesn't work, Miss Manners suggests cutting the ration.

The way to give someone the smallest fraction of attention short of cutting him, which would be insulting, is to stare at him with a blank smile while he talks and, when he pauses for an answer, to say apologetically, "Oh, I'm sorry, I wasn't following you; I'm thinking about my work." After he repeats his remarks, you repeat yours. You may have several rounds of this at first, but Miss Manners promises that it will take the fun out of his giving you advice.

Bossing the Boss

DEAR MISS MANNERS:

As a senior manager in an office, I receive many employee visitors throughout the day. I encourage employees to stop by as I have an open-door policy.

As most of these visits are impromptu, I am usually in the middle of a project or other task and have many documents on my desk. I am surprised at how many people will ask about the documents on my desk! Just today, as I was working on a confidential acquisition, a coworker stopped by, saw the document on my desk, and started quizzing me on what I was working on.

Miss Manners will not be happy to hear that my response was a question also—"Do you have a habit of reading things on other people's desks?"

OK—I know I was wrong. Is there a better response? Not only is this not their business, in many cases information needs to be confidential.

GENTLE READER:

Shut the door.

Miss Manners realizes how shocking a shut-door policy appears to those who believe in the non-hierarchal workplace in spite of the obvious fact that there is no such thing. But your open-door policy isn't working. It is not a defense of this frank but rude snooping to point out that you are encouraging your employees to ignore boundaries.

The simple act of knocking reminds people that you are working, and makes your willingness to stop and listen to them all the more gratifying. It also gives you time to put your blotter on top of confidential papers.

DEAR MISS MANNERS:

I employ 5 people in a small manufacturing setting. I encourage my employees to be friendly and have no problem with them talking during work or listening to the radio with their ear buds.

During the course of the day, I have occasional questions regarding the workflow or job completion. I will walk into the manufacturing area, and if I determine that the conversation is of a personal nature, I will politely stop the conversation and ask the business question at hand.

One of my employees has complained that I am being rude and ill-mannered when I stop their conversation. She feels that I should allow then to complete their personal chatter and when they are finished, I can speak to them.

My feeling is that this is my time and I pay the salary. I think I am being very generous with allowing them to chatter about personal things during the day. BUT. When I have business to conduct all should come to a stop and the business should be taken care of.

Am I being ill-mannered to expect that the workday is to come first? Let me know your thoughts.

GENTLE READER:

Your employees have gone from friendly to cheeky, is what Miss Manners thinks. That is the danger of slipping from a professional demeanor into one where people feel there is no hierarchy, and that their leisure should be respected.

Professional manners require attending to business when there is work to be done, and not keeping the boss waiting. The sooner you explain that to your employees, the better. And never mind whether they grouse about it—you are supposed to be their boss, not their buddy.

Ring and Wrong

DEAR MISS MANNERS:

One of my coworkers will often stand next to me while I am taking a phone call and wait for me to finish so that she can speak with me. Although business-related, I feel very uncomfortable with her listening to my every word and staring at me whilst I finish my business call.

If I look at her to acknowledge that she is waiting, she tries to whisper her message to me while I am still trying to take the business call. Then I end up not fully hearing either message. She can see that I am occupied and I feel that she should send me an email or come back. The question she is waiting to ask me is usually of very low importance.

How do I handle this tactfully? I have tried ignoring her behavior until the client is off the phone, but she still tries to get my attention.

GENTLE READER:

Do you have a swivel chair?

The polite "Go away; I'm busy" signal is a regretful smile with an optional shrug of the shoulders to indicate that you will be occupied for a while, so there is no point in waiting. But you have informed Miss Manners that your coworker waits anyway, and doesn't just wait quietly, but acts as if you were free to talk to her.

Here is where the swivel chair comes in: After having indicated your helplessness in responding while you are on the telephone, you can swivel around so that your back is toward the entrance, presuming that your colleague has done the right thing and left.

DEAR MISS MANNERS:

When I call another doctor, regardless of seniority or which of us or our clients are benefiting, I am there when the call is placed, and I will stand and wait if necessary (always with something to do during the interim). We professionals cannot know when we are interrupting, so it seems most polite to be there when the callee arrives.

Unfortunately, many of my colleagues don't feel the same way. I am frequently called to the phone by some other doctor's or some lawyer's secretary, who then says, "Please hold." I protest and don't usually hold, but rather put my secretary back on the line, or leave it on speakerphone in another room.

My number one priority is to my patients who are with me, and who need my time and undivided attention. But even after my secretary advises theirs that she is going to have to pull me out of a patient-examining room if it's so urgent, they are never ready.

GENTLE READER:

Miss Manners commends you for your convictions, and would like to urge you to have the courage that goes with them.

Teach your secretary the phrase, "I'm sorry, but he's with a patient."

What another doctor or lawyer calls "urgent" probably means urgent to that very doctor or lawyer, which is not a designation that you need accept. Unnecessarily declaring urgency is unfortunately a hallmark of those professions, to which you are a welcome exception. A doctor who had a life-or-death patient standing by who could only be saved by your telephone advice would surely say so.

When you are in your office, the solutions you suggest—putting on your secretary, or leaving the call on a speaker telephone while you do other work—are even kinder than the one Miss Manners has been known to employ. She says, "Please tell him that I'm so sorry I answered the telephone at an inconvenient time," and ties up the busy person's line no longer.

DEAR MISS MANNERS:

What is a practical and "proper" way for a doctor to respond when a patient, or in my case, a parent of a patient, initiates a cell phone call, responds to a ring, or continues a cell phone conversation while I'm in the exam room. I'm sure neither physical violence nor a lecture on manners is in order.

GENTLE READER:

The last Miss Manners checked, the Hippocratic oath precluded doctors' using violence to teach their patients manners. So, for that matter, does the Etiquettic oath.

What you can do is to stop the examination and use the time to take or return your own telephone calls, something Miss Manners trusts you would never do while seeing a polite patient. If you are challenged, you should reply that you are waiting until the patient or parent was free to pay attention to the examination.

How Right Is the Customer?

DEAR MISS MANNERS:

I grew up in the era when a motto of the retail business world was "The Customer Is Always Right." Naturally, that was not literally true, but at least it suggested that the customer deserved courtesy and attention, within reason.

I always become annoyed when I reach the cashier in a checkout line and find the clerk busily conversing with his or her colleague in the next aisle. Occasionally, my temper gets the best of me and I lecture the person (usually young) along the lines of, "I hate to be the one to point this out to you, but we are transacting business here which involves my purchases and my money, and it is extremely discourteous of you to be conversing past me with your neighbor as though I were not present."

I feel a little foolish when I let myself go that far, but at the same time, I feel that this is something that needs to be "corrected," as we used to say in the South of "correcting" misbehaving children.

I don't feel that this is serious enough to justify a formal complaint to the manager, who would then chastise the offending clerk: I think the clerk is usually unaware that there is anything wrong with his behavior. Do you have any suggestions about handling this situation without compromising one's own dignity and sense of propriety, but at the same time, without suffering in silence?

GENTLE READER:

Naturally it is not always true that the customer is always right, but it is not surprising, considering that this is not properly your job, that you got it a bit muddled. Your lecture suggests to Miss Manners that the situation would be fine—never mind the sordid matter of actually selling goods, or the impatience of those behind you—if only the two clerks included you in their conversation.

But suffering in silence is not the only alternative. If you don't want to hand the situation over to the person whose job it is to train and supervise the help, then voice the legitimate demand of the customer, which is, "Can you help me, please?"

Should this be ignored, then another version of it, "Is there anyone here who can help me?" ought to be made audibly enough to wake up your clerk, attract a more conscientious one, or be overheard by the manager.

DEAR MISS MANNERS:

I'm a compounding pharmacist (making custom medications "from scratch"; our pharmacy specializes in hormone replacement), and many of our clients tell me that I'm skilled at explaining their therapy (how much to use, what kind of symptoms to watch for, etc.). They're so impressed that they tell their friends—who then, often without getting a prescription, call and want me to spend work time discussing their symptoms, at length.

I don't want to upset them—they need help, and also might be potential clients—but my boss is paying me to mix and explain prescriptions, not to chat. How might I gently dissuade those who seek free advice on my boss's time?

GENTLE READER:

The advice you must dispense to such callers will help you, as well as them. It will save you not only time, but ethical distress.

Miss Manners would think that explaining the proper use of medications with your clients is one thing, and having medical discussions with strangers who tell you their symptoms over the telephone is quite another. The quick and helpful advice she recommends, therefore, is "Ask your doctor."

Avoiding the Customer

DEAR MISS MANNERS:

I have a photography studio in an affluent, highly populated area on a highly trafficked road. We pay high rent so new people will see our store and come in.

I try to work by appointment, so people get special attention and aren't treated badly because of the chaos that happens when people come by whenever they find it momentarily convenient. I'm not talking about new customers, but about people who've been here before and have been exposed to the way we work.

Am I a dinosaur? Does having a storefront mean that I have to put in a "take a number" system?

I've chosen not to hire someone to answer phones and do things like telling people to wait, but some customers refuse to cooperate and come when they choose. Do you think it's being unrealistic to try to build a business using personal attention, without hiring so many people that prices become prohibitive?

GENTLE READER:

Wait a minute. Nobody answers the telephone to take appointments, and yet you can't have people dropping in while you're working. And you have set things up to attract inquiries from strangers, but either can't deal with their inquiries, or are willing to do so at the expense of those who are there by appointment. But you are not willing to deal with your old customers who drop by.

Miss Manners is not complaining about the contradictions. She just wants to make sure she understands them. And what you want from her is a way to deal with these people when you are not free to do so yourself, and yet cannot hire someone else to do so.

Okay, sure.

You must cultivate a manner that says, "I'm thrilled to see you, but torn apart by the fact that I can't stop and help you because, as you see, I give everybody who has an appointment my full attention." Lots of hand-wringing and oh-dearing will help.

A rapid-fire dialogue, along the lines of "Oh, how nice to see you, but oh, dear, I've got someone with me now, can't you come back in a couple of hours so I can really have some time with you, or would it be better if we set a time another day, when would be good for you?" shouldn't take too long, especially if you say it all run together like that.

Be sure you insist that they either set an appointment or let you call them when you are free. Provided you seem devastated not to be able to accommodate them, short of actually dropping a live patron in order to attend to them, you will engage their sympathies in your plight.

Then apologize. That's right—apologize even though you did nothing wrong, and you think they did. While taking the form of an apology, it will really be a lesson: "I'm so sorry to have made you come back; I know how valuable your time is. Next time, if you just leave me a phone message when you want to come in, I'll get right back to you, and then I'll be able to devote myself to your sitting without any interruptions."

LIVING "ON CALL"

DEAR MISS MANNERS:

I have taken a job in which I must spend one out of three weeks "on call" twenty-four hours a day. I work with computers in a context that has life-or-death consequences, so when I am paged, I must drop everything and work immediately, usually for an hour or more at a time.

This only happens once or twice in an average one-week shift, but is so disruptive that I have stopped accepting engagements of any kind during these weeks. I will still invite friends to my home for a meal or games, but only with their understanding that I may be paged, somewhat like how I might let a good friend visit when I am sick.

Some friends have said I am going too far, isolating myself socially for fear of a page which, after all, most likely will not come. They urge me to come to restaurants or movies or even game nights, saying they will understand if I have to rush away. I think this would be intolerably rude, even if my friends say it is fine. What are your thoughts?

GENTLE READER:

Is there anyone, other than Miss Manners, who does not consider himself or herself to be on call all the time? The excuse of expecting an emergency summons from work or family is now so widespread that she wonders how the entire population manages to live in this state of permanent anxiety.

In the meantime, much of business and personal life has been damaged, as those supposedly engaged in one are on alert to drop everything on command from the other. So Miss Manners congratulates you on refusing to contribute to this. It strikes her that you have made a sensible accommodation to the situation. Your friends may claim not to mind if you suddenly exit from restaurants (what do they do with the food you ordered and the bill?), movie theaters (where you would disrupt others in your row), or game nights (where conclusions might be drawn between your losing and your leaving), but this tolerance may not last.

If they but knew it, it is more of an act of friendship to be able to give them your full attention when you can.

DEAR MISS MANNERS:

Help! My husband's employer expects him to be on call 365 days a year! (My husband works in fleet maintenance, and none of the calls are urgent.) What are some reasonable guidelines here? Is the phone on during sex? Is the phone on when one is dining at a friend's house? How about movies, restaurants, etc.? What about the phone itself? Is the matter life and death, or can it wait its course and be handled during normal working hours? What are some reasonable guidelines as the lines of distinction between work, family, and home become increasingly blurred?????

GENTLE READER:

If a family member is in a business in which he or she must be on call, the others must make some accommodations, but surely not to the extent of surrendering any possibility of having a peaceful private life. The worker's accommodation is to set aside sacred family time, such as refusing to be interrupted during the, ah, dinner hour. Such a job also limits attending social events to occasions where it is possible to be summoned and to slip away without disrupting the event; this can probably be taken care of with vibrating telephones, aisle seats, and attending only large, unseated parties.

The hard question is what to do when an employer insists unreasonably on accessibility that is ruinous to private life, both domestic and social. Miss Manners understands that it may not be easy to walk away from a job, and that families sometimes have to make sacrifices. She only asks that no one involved be deluded enough about such indentured labor as to imagine it feasible as more than a stopgap measure, much less that it gives off a whiff of glamour, power, and importance.

DEAR MISS MANNERS:

A person who is slightly above me on the supervisory chain (meaning she isn't a boss but she can affect our budget), has the bad habit of dropping by and interrupting our already short lunchtime to talk business. I have said something nicely but she doesn't seem to get the hint that we don't wish to be interrupted. Any suggestions?

GENTLE READER:

Why are you hinting? Why aren't you saying something?

Although it is advisable to demonstrate flexibility about hours and dedication to the job to one's superiors, nobody is high enough on the chain to abolish lunchtime.

One solution is to go out to lunch, because people who eat at their desks appear to be so over-zealous that they would rather not take a break. Those who skip eating but use the time to do something else, such as woolgathering, are indistinguishable from on-duty workers.

Miss Manners doesn't believe you should be driven to change your habits just to claim the break to which you are entitled. She suggests you convey both your dedication to the job and your dedication to lunch by saying, "I was just on my lunch break but I'd be glad to talk about this now, if you like, and take my lunch break when we're finished."

FRIENDLY NUISANCES

DEAR MISS MANNERS:

I am a street musician who entertains tourists and locals, and I wish you would let people know about busker etiquette.

I have made many friends over the years, and they often stroll by as I sing folk songs and play guitar. I don't mean to sound unappreciative, but it is difficult to perform when a friend stops to say "Hi" right during a song. Some go on and on, telling me all that is new in their lives! I stand there helpless and frustrated, as I see my customers wander off.

Friends should wave or say "Hi" quickly, and then move on. They could drop a business card in the hat with a short note—"Can we get together for coffee later?"—and remember that every little tip helps. And they should never, never let a child harass a performer.

GENTLE READER:

Happy as she is to pass on your eminently reasonable rules of busker etiquette (and secretly thrilled to find a new subdivision of her field), Miss Manners suspects that the very informality of your form of entertainment will always encourage people of good will—as opposed to those nasties who allow their children to harass anyone, under any circumstances—to feel that you are socially approachable during your performances.

Therefore, Miss Manners considers you in need of polite methods of reacting to mid-performance pleasantries. First, you must cultivate an agreeable expression (a fleeting one, that will end the encounter without interrupting your music) that clearly says, "I'm afraid I can't talk to you right now." The look to practice is the one that comes naturally to polite people who are addressed while their mouths are full of food.

Miss Manners trusts you, as a performer, to master this for yourself. The basic idea is that the upper half of the face shows regret (furrowed brow, sad eyes), while the lower half registers friendly helplessness (closed-mouth half-smile).

For those who persist, you should have a tuneful line of greeting-and-goodbye (along the lines of "Great to see you, talk to you later," only perhaps rhyming) that you can insert into the music without derailing your performance.

Miss Manners understands that this may be a nuisance to you. But she feels obliged to remind you that being in the folk music business involves dealing with feedback from the folks, and that there are worse reactions one can get from them than the desire to be friends.

DEAR MISS MANNERS:

I am a nurse at a local hospital. We have open visitation. I sometimes have to work my necessary care around visitors. Patients will not get their proper out-of-bed time, assistance with walks, and bathing. Many have had surgery and this is necessary.

Some find it rude that I interrupt their visits. I try and include the visitor when possible and work around them but some just don't get it and stay a long time. The patient feels rude in excusing themselves or is avoiding the activity required by the doctor. How do I handle this and remain courteous?

GENTLE READER:

If medical requirements did not trump social ones, polite people would be letting others choke to death rather than rudely laying hands on them.

But Miss Manners does not recognize a conflict between being courteous and being firm. The usual method is for the person in charge—and the patient is, at such time, in your charge—to say, "I'm afraid I'll have to ask you to wait in the lounge" for however long is necessary. Doing so relieves the patient from having to dismiss his or her guests. Should anyone argue, you should say, "I'm sure you want what is best for him. We all want him to get well so you can have your visits elsewhere."

DEAR MISS MANNERS:

I work graveyards and often receive calls early in the morning from persons who don't know I sleep during those hours. I must keep the phone on for emergencies as I am on call. Sometimes when people call, they ask, "Did I wake you?"

Saying no is a lie. I have said "Yes, but it's okay." The person often apologizes and feels bad. I don't mean to make them feel bad. And saying something like, "I am glad you called, what's up?" seems like you are ignoring the person's question. None of these seem like good responses. What would you suggest?

GENTLE READER:

Having worked the graveyard shift herself (although not in a graveyard), Miss Manners is afraid that you will have to learn to protect yourself. Nine-to-five people have trouble getting their minds around the notion that people should never be luxuriating in bed on weekday mornings, even if they only just got off work.

So ignoring the question and pretending to welcome the intrusion is not going to disabuse them of the idea that they picked a good time to call. At the same time, you don't want to be rude, Miss Manners is gratified to hear.

Your answer "Yes, but it's okay" is fine. So are their apologies and moment of feeling bad. If you go on talking to them pleasantly, the bad feelings will not reach nightmarish proportions, but be just strong enough to remind them not to do it again.

Helpful Interruptions

DEAR MISS MANNERS:

I am in a technical profession (software), and some subjects require an extensive explanation to express completely. Sometimes when listening to a colleague give a long bit on a tricky subject, I realize that they have the wrong idea about something and I interrupt them before they can complete their thought. I do this because I want to save them the trouble of a five- or ten-minute explanation (sometimes complete with drawings on a whiteboard)! Here's an example:

Colleague: ". . . so you see, the best choice in this case is to put the services on the same machine as the database. Let me explain how this is done . . ."

Me: "Hold on a moment. You see, the client has stipulated that the two cannot reside on the same machine."

I've only ever had one colleague complain about this; ironically, she had a habit of interrupting me while I was talking, too. I never took any offense, but one time she went out of her way to discuss this with me at length. After that, I would let her finish her statements and wait for a half of a second before speaking out of respect for her wishes.

Is it always rude to interrupt people when they are talking? I usually let people finish but when I sense the conversation is veering off on a tangent I will sometimes interrupt them. What does Miss Manners say?

GENTLE READER:

Are you finished?

Miss Manners does not want to be accused of interrupting you, even though there are times when it is not impolite to do so. When the building is on fire, for example.

In the normal give-and-take of conversation, chiming in, briefly, with relevant comments or questions, is a show of interest, compared to simply sitting through a monologue and stealing glances at one's email.

In general, at a business meeting, speakers should be allowed to make their reports without interruptions and take questions when they conclude. However, saving time is also a valuable contribution. It is best done in the form of a question, "Excuse me, but didn't the client stipulate . . . ?"

UNHELPFUL TACTICS

DEAR MISS MANNERS:

Has the etiquette of the workplace changed in the last few years, or is my office some weird aberration? My coworkers think nothing of playing loud music at their desks, forcing everyone in the vicinity to share in the "entertainment."

They are allegedly "creatives," and it could be that this atmosphere of unregulated chaos stimulates them. But my work requires concentration and I can't drop what I'm doing because some rude so-and-so has decided it's time to entertain the entire floor.

Some of the music isn't bad, but I'd rather hear it in a different setting, and much of what they play is incredibly grating.

Either way, I was taught you just don't do that in the workplace. You wear headphones or you adjust the volume to a level that cannot be heard outside of your cubicle. It's annoying to be forced to listen to scratchy, distorted tunes from the other side of the room. I won't even get into their use of speakerphones, their lingering "hanging around" gabfests, or the loud video games they play. What astounds me is that I'm the only one who seems to mind. My coworkers are mostly in their 20s and I'm a few years (decades) older.

Are these people rude, clueless dolts to whom the concept of "putting yourself in someone else's shoes" is completely foreign, or is it a generational thing? Have these 20-somethings grown up in a world so full of distracting noise and disregard for personal space that this is second nature to them?

My bosses don't seem to mind, either—they do it too! I'm forced to wear headphones most of the day, but that's a nuisance, and the only music I can really work to is commercial-free, lyric-free classical or jazz. Please advise or supply a pithy reprimand I can discreetly clip to the wall.

GENTLE READER:

Let's see if Miss Manners understands you correctly:

You are the oldest person in the office. You are the only person in the office who does not like the music. And you want to issue a public challenge sneering at behavior that the boss not only condones but personally enjoys.

Are you hoping for early retirement?

Miss Manners does believe that even one objection should be enough to curb intrusive behavior in a situation where people are required to be together. But she is not ignorant of the difficulty of taking on an entire office that is otherwise in tune with one another's wishes.

Pithy is not the way to go, even if Miss Manners knew what on earth you meant by doing this discreetly. Do you imagine they won't know who it is? Or that they will be covered with shame? Pleading would be more like it. Go to the boss with the apologetic admission that you have trouble concentrating during the music, and the request that earphones might be used. As much as he may appreciate the music, he probably appreciates productivity more.

CHAPTER 8

Stop Asking Me How I'm Doing

You inform your spouse that your boss is an idiot.

You warn your colleagues, over a drink after work, that if the pace does not slow down, mistakes are going to be made.

You post on your blog that what the company says it's putting in the product and what it is actually putting in the product are not the same.

You pin a jocular note on the bulletin board announcing that you are going to blow up the building.

Well, if you didn't do any of these things, Miss Manners knows that you thought about it. Just about every employee is tempted over the course of a career and perhaps over the course of a day.

Which ones would land you in the personnel department and which ones would land you in the local precinct, depends on the context. Whether the unannounced ingredient is formaldehyde in the milk, oregano in the secret recipe, or alien broadcasts in the radio transmission will matter, and not just to yourself. If your construction company was hired to demolish abandoned offices, blowing up the building might be appropriate. If the mistake you are worried about is going to happen at a nuclear power plant, that may be a bit different than if you work for a sports magazine.

But what about the context of the remark itself? It is reasonable for an employer to expect loyalty from the employees—at least loyalty to the company, which is not the same thing as personal loyalty to the boss—but it is also true that an employee is not expected to surrender his opinions.

Private expressions of dissatisfaction are acceptable; public ones are only so in exceptional circumstances and even then, there are rules. The worker who blows the whistle on a manufacturer who is endangering children is a hero. The one who tells potential customers not to buy his employer's product because it's a waste of money is probably not. Opinions may vary about the worker who discovers that the manufacturing process is contaminating the milk and mentions this to the media before telling the boss, though probably not the boss's opinion.

The demarcation between public and private was clearer when there was an office door. Not every minute spent at work might have been spent on work, but the assumption was there. Cubicle "farms," "open offices," and lunch rooms—not to mention long hours—at work, and telecommuting, sales jobs, and social media bloggers off-site, have made it less clear what is on, and what off, the clock.

But the basic distinction remains. Posting a screed against your boss on a social media site—and then complaining that the information became public only because the site changed its privacy policies—will get you nowhere with either your boss or Miss Manners. If you commit a foolish criticism to paper and drop it on the street, you have only yourself to blame.

DEAR MISS MANNERS:

We've all heard about people being fired for ranting online about their bosses, coworkers, company policy. Well, a friend of mine ranted about her F-ing boss on Facebook. Her boss is my mother. I don't want to jeopardize this person's career. What to do?

GENTLE READER:

Jeopardize this person's career. Your mother may decide to be merciful, but Miss Manners assures you that no civilized person can allow his or her mother to be publicly insulted, deservedly or not.

DEAR MISS MANNERS:

Last week, I yelled at my secretary. She got upset and she went home early. Yesterday I bought her some begonias at the grocery store. The flowers cost $7.99. As of today, she has not sent me a thank-you card. Is she out of line?

GENTLE READER:

Why, the hussy—not to come blubbering with gratitude, and after you'd invested so much thought and money, too. Are you planning to yell at her for it?

Miss Manners must warn you not to expect gratitude, as your flowers were an apology rather than a present. They should have been accompanied by an explicit note of apology. Even had you done this, the most you can hope for is that she will accept that apology and refrain from telling the travel agent that you prefer the middle seat.

Whiny Colleagues

DEAR MISS MANNERS:

I have a coworker who said, in an office meeting, that she "hates me and does not wish to work with me." When questioned as to why and what I did to bring this on, her reply was that she does not like my behavior. I feel this is causing undue strife for the entire office. What would you suggest to elevate some of the tension?

GENTLE READER:

The tension sounds high enough already. It's a good thing Miss Manners is too polite to wonder whether your little slip hints that you might secretly like to elevate the tension into violence.

Mind you, she doesn't blame you for feeling that way, even though she won't let you act on it. For anyone to make such a statement, especially at an office meeting, is breathtakingly rude. But it is not a personal problem, however personal it feels to have someone announce that she hates you. It is a personnel problem. This person can hate you all she wants, but should not be allowed to let it interfere with the work of the office or to stir up trouble by airing these feelings.

Apparently the person running the meeting did not do the proper thing, which would have been to reprimand the complainer for engaging in insults rather than airing her grievance civilly. You need to talk to someone with an interest in maintaining professional behavior and the authority to enforce it. As dispassionately as possible (it doesn't do to violate professional behavior when you are complaining that someone else has), you should report the facts and express a desire to know what the problem is so that it can be solved and everybody can again cooperate to get the work done.

DEAR MISS MANNERS:

I'm the head of a marketing division at a software company. My coworkers are a collegial and professional bunch—all except for a group of obnoxious young engineers. When we meet to talk about a campaign to promote a new software release, they'll roll their eyes at our ideas and give exasperated answers to our questions. One engineer even went so far as to call us "stupid" for not understanding his explanation of a new technology.

The engineers do great work, but their behavior is having a lousy impact on morale. I've asked the engineering chief to speak to his staff, but he just laughs and says that's just the way programmers are. Should I speak to his boss about this?

GENTLE READER:

Not with that argument. Miss Manners is afraid you have already given far too many people the opportunity to discuss the dull-wittedness of the marketing division.

She delicately suggests that it is time to retaliate. But as she forbids countering rudeness with more rudeness, you must do so in a businesslike manner.

First drop that complaint about not understanding the engineers' explanations. Then drop the argument that their manner is bad for morale. The engineers are having a fine time watching your bewilderment and signaling one another how much stupider than they the rest of the world is. Their morale couldn't be better.

But we can fix that. The complaint you need to lodge is that the engineers, talented as they are, unfortunately lack communication skills. Their ideas are good, but they have difficulty expressing them, and when attempts are made to help them, they turn defensive. Sometimes, when their efforts to be articulate fail, they start acting childish. Notice that this not only flips the question of who seems slow, but heads off the response that it is others' fault for not understanding (because that sounds defensive) or ridicule (because that has been defined as childishness).

Whiny Clients

DEAR MISS MANNERS:

It is in desperation that I turn to you to teach proper etiquette to the 20+ crowd for dealing with problems they have with businesses they patronize.

I refer to the all-too-common practice of leaving the place in a huff, rushing to the computer, and yelping about the experience over the Internet. The resulting scathing reviews sharply cut into the business's customers and revenues. The damage can be severe. Loyal and appreciative customers can do nothing to repair the victim's reputation.

One extremely popular Web site makes all its money by charging businesses $300 a month both to select which reviews come first on its site and to answer the charges of the negative reviewer. There are reports that businesses who refuse to pay find the good reviews vanishing from their sites and bad reviews taking their place.

I, personally, am horrified by the bad reviews I see. The revered and highly respected ob-gyn who successfully steered me through an extremely difficult twin pregnancy was given a one-star review by someone who visited his office once.

She announced to him that she had decided not to have children. He engaged her in what he thought was harmless banter. She flounced out and gave him a scathing review. He lost patients. When I related this story to strangers at a coffee shop, they immediately knew who the doctor was and were amazed that he had a bad review from anyone!

Professional restaurant critics visit restaurants several times with friends before they write their review. While not every review is glowing, all reviews are polite and give credit to the business for knowing its trade. People who expect and deserve good service from the business they patronize politely bring any shortcomings to the attention of the owner/manager and give them a chance to rectify the situation. They do not yelp!

GENTLE READER:

As your one example is on behalf of your doctor, Miss Manners will assume that you do not have a professional interest in suppressing complaints. Those who do are now taking it to the courts.

But is she mistaken in detecting an edge against all who use this method of making their grievances heard? She does agree that dissatisfied customers and clients should first complain calmly to the person or business itself. Reputable businesspeople have thanked her for doing so, always saying how much they prefer the chance to make amends instead of losing patronage without knowing why.

But not every person or company is conscientious—or even reachable. Reviews have been a much-needed outlet for those who have been given the Your-Call-Is-Important-to-Us runaround. Besides, such sites contain recommendations as well as complaints. Why don't you write one for your doctor? Although Miss Manners considers it injudicious, at best, to banter with a patient over an important and emotional issue, she might be swayed by strong evidence of professional competence.

DEAR MISS MANNERS:

I work in my cousin's grocery store in the cashier position. We get customers coming in, purchasing a product, and then complaining about how expensive it is. They then proceed to say how they could get it cheaper some place else, or just down the block.

As the cashier and working for a relative, what should I say or do? I could simply ignore them, but the urge to say, "Why don't you go there and buy it, if it's cheaper there?" gets stronger and stronger. I've had it up to my head with this kind of customer.

GENTLE READER:

What you are listening to is not anything so sensible as an evaluation of competitive commercialism as simple grousing. Miss Manners doesn't blame you for being annoyed, but believes anything so reasonable as arguing would be pointless, as well as bad for business.

Try replying cheerfully, "Well, we certainly appreciate your patronage," as if the store had been complimented by these remarks. Indeed, it has been. If your customers are really willing to pay higher prices at your store, it must be that the atmosphere or service is better. Surely you want to encourage, rather than dispel, that possibility.

DEAR MISS MANNERS:

For the second time in as many months, I have been informed by a local doctor's office (two different doctors' offices on the two occasions) that my appointment "has been changed." Not "We regret to inform you that Dr. Schmoe will be unable to keep the appointment that you had; can you come in at 4 on Friday instead?" but "Your new appointment is at 4 on Friday."

I don't know about you, but the way they have presumed to word that message makes me feel greasy all over. It is important to me that an appointment is negotiated between the patient and the doctor's office, not assigned by the latter. All of us have other things we have to do besides suiting a doctor's convenience.

Three questions: 1) Do you agree that the doctor's office is unnecessarily rude? 2) Has this rudeness already spread all over the country? 3) Will you please tell them to cut it out?

GENTLE READER:

1) Yes. 2) Yes. 3) Yes.

Whiny Friends

DEAR MISS MANNERS:

I love my job as a high school literature teacher. One can hardly begin to create a complete list of why the job is so amazing.

Yet in 12 years of teaching, I regularly encounter two comments when people find out my profession. They either cringe ("Wow—why would you ever want to deal with brats every day?") or think they're handing me a compliment ("It must be so great to have the summers off").

If I were to deal with brats every day, I'd go into a different profession. I also doubt they understand that most of us don't get paid over the two-month summer break even though we continue to prepare for the following year. How should one best respond to these remarks and transition into some topic that is a bit more pleasing all around?

GENTLE READER:

There is no stopping people from making silly remarks about one's profession—any profession—as Miss Manners knows from constant personal experience.

The simplest way is to answer with a weak smile and say, "Tell me about what you do." No explanation or transition necessary. But if you are really fed up with those who remark about brats, you can say sympathetically, "Did you have a hard time in high school?"

DEAR MISS MANNERS:

I work for a service-industry company whose presence in my region of the country, while not a complete monopoly, is definitely the majority of the market. We have service failures on occasion, and when I'm out socially with friends, their experiences with these failures will come up as a part of conversation.

As a front-line employee, I empathize with their difficulties and try to get them pointed to the person in the department that may provide them with some recompense for their inconvenience. My quandary is with one particular person in my social group. This is the spouse of a good friend, and he seems to take pleasure in basically complaining. He never seems interested in the solutions I try to provide or in lodging his complaint with the department responsible for handling service failures. I'm starting to dread times when I have to encounter him.

GENTLE READER:

Do the people whom you do help, when out socially, reciprocate? Do they give you free legal or plumbing advice, or troubleshoot for you at their airlines, tax bureaus, or wherever they are employed?

Even so, Miss Manners would not envy your social life. It must be tiresome to be forever on duty, which is why it is rude for those people to corner you on your off-hours. She commends you for your patience in not chucking the lot of them. As for the persistent complainer, it is time to say, "It's a long time now that you've been unhappy with our services and with my attempts to help you. We'll be sorry to lose you as a customer, but since we can't please you, you really ought to take your business elsewhere."

DEAR MISS MANNERS:

My husband is a low-level worker for a high-profile company whose legal woes have been in the news a lot lately. I am very disappointed that the media frenzy surrounding the case has given a public image of the company that is really very inaccurate.

Friends, acquaintances, and even strangers are getting misinformed ideas about the company, and are consequently transferring those ideas onto us personally—as if my husband, specifically, were responsible for any alleged wrongdoing that upper management engaged in, or that we have somehow profited from ill-gotten gains. I'm actually starting to feel like I should feel personally guilty for what's happening—as if the company was poisoning schoolchildren and we were the ones handing it out!

Even if the company did do something wrong, it was very mild, and we had nothing to do with it. How can I explain that we, and the company, are not what we're being made out to be? How do I deal with endless questions about the case? Everyone I talk to wants to know what the "insider's" view is.

We haven't lost any friends out of the deal—especially as many of our friends are also coworkers—but those not close to the case still pepper us with questions. I don't want to be rude, as it would make things worse, yet even the bit of defense I've engaged in seems to make people think we're hiding something or doing unsavory spin control.

GENTLE READER:

Mild jokes, airy evasions, and professions of ignorance are what Miss Manners usually recommends for dealing with intrusive questions. And she keeps hoping this approach will replace the currently more popular convention (snarling "Mind your own business!"). The defense of being just a little guy doing his job without understanding what the big guys are doing got rather a bad name from World War II.

Serious accusations that one is practicing or countenancing dishonesty should not be brushed off as mere nosiness. But you should also be careful that you are not forcing that meaning onto straightforward inquiries about the company's justification or onto jokes. To cover all these possibilities, you should say with gentle reproof, "I'm sure you didn't mean to suggest that my husband would do anything shady."

OVERHEARD INFORMATION

DEAR MISS MANNERS:

Today I received an email from a business associate. Upon opening the email and reading the first sentence I quickly determined that the content was very personal (medical stuff) and not meant for me. With some effort I overcame my curiosity and deleted the email without reading the rest of the lengthy message or looking at any of the attached photos.

So far I have chosen to ignore the email. But the sender will most likely realize her mistake at some time. I'd like to assure her that I respected her privacy (as best as I could), but I hate to cause her any undue embarrassment.

Should I have immediately replied that I apparently received an email not meant for me so I deleted it without reading it, and thought she'd like to know so that she could send it to the proper recipient? (Is that even believable?) Or is it best to just pretend it never happened?

GENTLE READER:

Miss Manners believes you. But sadly she believes you are right in suspecting that no one else will. What you might say that is more plausible is, "I believe I got an email from you, but I couldn't open it, and now it's gone." The "couldn't" here refers to your high standard of morality.

DEAR MISS MANNERS:

Would you be kind enough to instruct physicians to close the doors to their waiting and examining rooms?

There is little else so disconcerting as to attempt to bury one's ears in a magazine while a room full of patients are subjected to voices discussing intimate details of medical procedures and secretaries ask for your diagnosis *en pleine vue*.

GENTLE READER:

Miss Manners can think of something much more disconcerting than attempting to bury one's ears, etc. People in waiting rooms are either bored or worried or both, and badly in need of amusement.

Her idea of disconcerting would be to walk through a waiting room on the way out and hear your doctor talking to the next patient—and thus be hit with the realization that everyone there had heard all about you.

Miss Manners hereby instructs physicians and their staffs in general to shut their doors, but she instructs you to notify yours in particular—immediately. Tell them it is an etiquette emergency.

DEAR MISS MANNERS:

Two years ago, my church announced that a counselor was available if anyone felt they needed personal, confidential counseling. My concern was that a dearly beloved "relative" was involved in drugs.

After a few sessions, I realized the counselor was not trained and not capable of helping me. He assured me that what I revealed would be held in strictest confidence.

Since that time, the man's wife has been greeting me at church functions with "How is your relative?" I am shocked that her husband betrayed my confidence and I refuse to shake her extended hand or answer her question.

She acts offended. What would be the most effective reply or action toward this unfeeling, crude and un-Christian person to put her in her place and let her know I am furious and disgusted with her and her husband for their unethical deportment?

GENTLE READER:

Miss Manners has no doubt that the person in question already knows that you are furious at her. That is why she acts offended.

Making her understand why would be considerably harder. Her husband was at least aware that it would be wrong to divulge what you told him, although he did it anyway. The wife's using this material for social conversation indicates that she may not even have known that her husband had violated the ethics of his position.

But making them understand this is not your job; it is the job of whoever has the authority to remove him from his position for this serious breach. Tell that person or board. Social snubs are no substitute for professional complaints.

DEAR MISS MANNERS:

I was recently at work and in the middle of a quick personal phone call. I was calling my doctor's office to get the results of a pregnancy test. A coworker was nearby so I tried to discreetly ask for my results, but I had to tell the nurse which "test result" I was talking about. The next day the woman had the nerve to tell me that she overheard my phone call and wanted to know if I "had good news."

I was so shocked that she would ask that I didn't know what to say. How could this type of situation be handled in the future?

GENTLE READER:

One way would be to make personal calls, particularly those of a sensitive nature, on your lunch hour instead of during work when other people are within hearing distance. But Miss Manners seems to be the only person who thinks of that.

That is the only way to protect your secret, even though politeness does require inadvertent eavesdroppers to pretend they haven't heard what was not intended for them. If you simply want to avoid discussion, you can do some pretending of your own.

Simply say, "I'm afraid I don't know what you're talking about," as a way of ending the conversation. Should anyone be so brash as to persist, you can gently explain that it is natural to misunderstand a telephone conversation when one only hears half of it.

FAILED NICENESS

DEAR MISS MANNERS:

Our company had one of those self-review days where we looked at where we had come financially and on a personnel basis, and where we were headed.

One of the senior officials rhymed off a group of newcomers to the company—getting one name wrong and missing another person altogether. This official then went on to praise a handful of people for their work, while neglecting others who had (in the estimation of a number of their colleagues) done work of at least equal caliber and ignoring the bulk of others who work truly hard every day.

There were special awards for outstanding work, and I don't think a single person begrudged anyone those citations. However, I think there should have been a better way before that to congratulate people without making anyone feel left out. As it was, a number of egos were crushed and feelings were hurt—unnecessarily, I think.

Am I right? What should the official have done? This is an annual affair, and I wouldn't want the same thing to be repeated.

GENTLE READER:

If there is anything more frightening in the ordinary workaday world than a boss trying to be cute, Miss Manners cannot imagine what it could be. Unless it is a boss being cute about people whose names he has not troubled to learn properly.

An annual review ought to be conducted seriously. Miss Manners sees nothing wrong with singling out certain workers for awards, although this, too, was botched if a substantial number of people feel that some outstanding work was ignored. And formal thanks should always be given to the workers as a whole.

But giving this event the atmosphere of a children's birthday party, ditty and all, creates the expectation that the point was to go around the room giving everyone a turn, and make everyone equally happy. That is properly the point of an office party, or better yet an announcement of bonuses or paid vacations, not of a review session.

DEAR MISS MANNERS:

My coworkers and I met a challenge put forth by my supervisor where she agreed to buy each of us an ice cream treat.

I am on a restricted diet that does not allow such types of food, and my supervisor is aware of this. When she asked me what flavor I wanted, I asked if I could have the money instead.

She said no, that she did not like that idea, so I went without the reward that everyone else received. She didn't offer me an alternate reward.

GENTLE READER:

Like what—a gold star on your report card?

Adults are supposed to understand a mild little joke when they hear one. Your supervisor did not mean to offer a serious incentive, or she could have given out bonuses. Ice cream was mentioned both because it makes the challenge sound like a children's game, and because it has little monetary value.

(There will now be a long pause while Miss Manners runs out to double-check the current price of an ice cream cone. Could it have turned into a serious investment since she last indulged? And then there will be a longer pause while she gets into the spirit of it and refuses to leave the ice cream parlor and go back to work.)

Where were we?

Oh, yes. At the time of the bargain, you could playfully have negotiated an equally token reward, by saying, for example, "What about a bagel for those of us who don't eat sweets?" But to demand compensation afterward is to indicate that you are seriously being childish, so to speak.

DEAR MISS MANNERS:

I am a sales representative and recently had a very uncomfortable situation arise when my manager accompanied me on a call. She "took the lead" with an important client of mine and was both pushy and rude to him.

He was gracious and told her plainly three times that he didn't like the way she was addressing him. The fourth time he politely ended the interview. I attempted to tone her down but was not successful.

I feel terrible about this—it was his office after all—and sent him a handwritten note of apology later that day. He and I have had a good relationship over several years and I do not want to see it suffer, although I'm afraid it may. Obviously I will never allow my manager to see him again, but is there anything else you would recommend that I do?

GENTLE READER:

Well, let's see. You attempted to protect your manager from the consequences of her own behavior. You apologized to the person she offended. And you are arranging to protect him from her in the future.

Miss Manners is not only impressed but certain that the client understands that far from its being your fault, you did everything you could to correct the situation. She trusts that you are not hankering to report your manager for bad behavior.

But you could do one more thing for Miss Manners. That would be to work in a half-apology for your manager—not defending her action, not even excusing it, but just offering the low-key suggestion that her manner belies her good intentions. Perhaps, as an etiquette bonus, it will also suggest to your client that you are tolerant and loyal, rather than righteous and given to tattling.

Gift Horses

DEAR MISS MANNERS:

At my husband's request, I sent a gift to his secretary. Although my husband told me that she thanked him, she never called me or sent me a thank-you note. This year, my husband would again like me to send her a gift, but I don't much feel like it. Am I being petty?

GENTLE READER:

Please be kind enough to indulge Miss Manners in imagining a purely hypothetical situation in which a gentleman requests his secretary to help him get a present for his wife.

There is no need to suppose that the gentleman Miss Manners has in mind is anything but devoted to his wife and eager to find something that will please her. It's just that he is suddenly pressed for time, finds that he is bad at selecting successful presents, admires his wife's taste but can't analyze what it is, remembers that his wife particularly admires his secretary's taste, or some combination of these. We'll even suppose that he understands that this is not a secretary's proper job but asks it as a favor.

This has nothing to do with your husband, of course. But do you think the wife would owe the secretary a formal letter of thanks (as opposed to a gracious but casual word of thanks dropped when the opportunity might present itself)?

Shouldn't it be the husband who gets the hugs and squeals of delight? Wasn't it his affection that the present symbolized even if he didn't do the actual shopping?

Miss Manners thinks it was generous of you to do your husband's office errand—as it would be for a secretary to do her boss's personal errand. Nevertheless, she maintains that your husband's present to his secretary is intended to symbolize his gratitude for her work and thus it comes from him. Your participation does not make you the secretary's co-boss any more than Miss Manners' hypothetical situation turns the secretary into a member of the family.

DEAR MISS MANNERS:

My husband has asked me to buy a present for his secretary, a woman who's been working in his office for about four months. I know that you are against giving money as a gift, but since I've never met this woman and know very little about her, I wondered if it would be polite to give her a gift certificate to a department store, where she can get anything she wants or needs?

GENTLE READER:

Miss Manners is grateful that you remember one half of her lesson about presents and money, but unfortunately it's the wrong half.

Yes, she is against giving money as a present to one's relatives and friends because symbolically it admits that one hasn't observed enough about that person to have a clue what to get, and isn't willing to put in the effort to find out.

But in the business world, you are not supposed to peep into people's lives and psyches. Even giving an employee a gift certificate to a department store presumes you know where she likes to shop. Tell your husband to use the money to give the secretary a bonus.

You are not the only person to get this backwards, but while friends and relatives should not be given money instead of presents, employees should not be given presents instead of money.

PAYING RESPECTS

DEAR MISS MANNERS:

I work in a 60-member assessor's office. Shortly after I started working there, my mother passed away. At that time the office failed to acknowledge this, not sending flowers or even a card.

Since that time, I have noticed that the office's policy is definitely to acknowledge employees' relatives' deaths, new babies, weddings, even recently the operation of an employee's husband was acknowledged with a card and flowers.

Should I see this as possibly a very negative comment on me by my office colleagues and seek employment elsewhere? Is it appropriate for me to refuse to sign cards, etc., for the other employees? I am very hurt and I must face these people every day.

GENTLE READER:

Now that you have been there longer, have you become aware of meetings in which employees' individual merits are weighed to determine whether they are worthy of receiving condolence or congratulatory cards?

Separate question: Have you noticed any small signs of inefficiency, such as are normal even in well-run organizations?

Miss Manners can assure you that what you perceive as an intentional slight was no such thing. As you have noticed, it is simply office policy to send cards. Her inescapable conclusion is that since you were a newcomer, they had not yet included you on the employee list, or they felt it was intrusive to offer sympathy to someone they didn't yet know. These would have been mistakes, but not insults.

DEAR MISS MANNERS:

I am getting ready to attend a memorial service for a coworker and have a question. This is an individual who worked for this organization for 18 years and she has many friends and close coworkers who still work here.

In preparation for the memorial service, a request was made by the Board of Directors to have special seating at the memorial service. None of them had a close relationship with the deceased. This seems rather insensitive to me or at least tacky. Why should attention be drawn to those who had no personal connection to the deceased? Their position within the organization would seem to have nothing to do with the purpose of the memorial service. What do you think?

GENTLE READER:

That you are missing the symbolism here—and the purpose of a memorial service is expressed through symbolism.

Indeed, the board of directors does have an important connection to the deceased. They represent the organization for which she worked for eighteen years. Miss Manners understands that you and the lady's friends are there to show your personal respect, but they are there to show the company's respect.

CHAPTER 9

Enough Is How Much?

As with all properly-reared ladies, Miss Manners was taught that it is vulgar to discuss money. Nowadays, she is probably the only person left whom you can count upon not to ask you how much you paid for your shoes or to announce what she paid for hers.

But incurably ladylike as she remains, she is quick enough to understand that this rule applies only to social manners, and that observing it professionally would bring the business world to a halt. Not everyone does. Many of those whose only party topic is money are strangely tongue-tied when it comes to negotiating salaries, raises, and prices. It is yet another of those modern reversals of context, whereby the social restriction shows up at work, while commercial conversation prevails on the social scene.

Gentlemen did not used to suffer from such timidity, having learned to dispense with manly frankness when entering the drawing room. Now that they are leery of being bested in social conversation by outspoken ladies, many have shifted that inhibition to the workplace. A surprising number of employees of both genders are voluntarily avoiding the topic of money for fear of being considered uncollegial.

Whereas formerly this delicacy was intended to charm the ladies, it now charms bosses. An atmosphere in which no one petitions for a raise is indeed collegial to those who might have to give one. And it is a fact of business life that in bad economic times, it is easier to replace workers.

Miss Manners has never asserted (as have some, in their desperation to peddle civility) that politeness in itself necessarily produces riches, any more than morality inevitably triumphs. But she does maintain that money matters may be asserted as forcefully and more successfully when they are not made offensively. That money should be clearly discussed in business does not justify yelling about it, except perhaps on the floor of the stock exchange.

But even in business, negotiation has its time and its place. It is acceptable to question the price in an antiques store or a car dealership, but not to try to wrangle a discount in the supermarket or on the bus. It takes two willing participants to conduct a negotiation, and either side can politely refuse.

Good will must be presumed. The party guest who has his facts wrong can be gently contradicted—and probably will be, with everyone whipping out telephones to check—but letting it go may do no harm and interfere less with dessert. The antiques dealer who refuses a price on the grounds that he is saving the toy car for his only son can be reminded that his son is old enough to borrow the keys to the real car.

Not so the boss who refuses a raise with the untrue assertion that colleagues in the office are receiving the same salary. Better to moan about the state of the business and the value of the employee. Letting the lie stand can have serious consequences. Paying with compliments is easier than bluntly refusing, and the wise employee memorizes the speech to repeat it when profits are up.

Getting One's Due

DEAR MISS MANNERS:

I am 15 years old and I babysit for a family. I like babysitting for them, and love the little girl, but lately they have started paying me much below minimum wage, like $4 a hour! Until I am 16, I want to babysit for extra money.

I would love to stay babysitting for them, but I don't feel it is worth my time if I don't get paid very well. How can I tell them to pay me more? This is my only job until I can get a real one, so I'm not making as much money as I would like to.

GENTLE READER:

Who is?

More to the point, you are not making what you reasonably expect to make. But evidently your employers do not realize that.

Miss Manners understands that you feel funny about mentioning what you charge because it seems rude. But the ban on discussing money matters does not apply to business. If you want to buy something, you want to be told what it costs. The next time these people call, you need only say politely, "I'd love to, but you should know that my rate is . . ." and give the amount.

DEAR MISS MANNERS:

The problem I am facing is that I dog-sit for people in my college community (professors, landlords, etc.) and know that I will, in all likelihood, have to continue dog-sitting when I graduate this spring with a BA in fashion, even if I can find a job.

While this doesn't bother me (sometimes I like dogs better than people), I face the question, "How much would you like to be paid?" I understand it's a very necessary question, but I never know what to say. I don't have a set price, and I'm willing to work around the budgets of people I know and like. I am never certain of any clients' finances, and I refuse to inquire.

I suppose I am stuck between setting a price and changing it for some, which may appear like I'm doing charity, or leaving payment open, where it might get around that I charge differently for different people, which would be just as bad, if not worse. I suppose it comes down to my looking for a polite and tactful way to ease into the subject of finances without offending, being underpaid, or appearing greedy.

GENTLE READER:

So there you are with an etiquette standoff, because you can't ask your clients about their financial situations and you also can't name a price, because it depends on what they can afford.

But meanwhile, the dogs are jumping about nervously near the front door, desperate to get out. Miss Manners will make haste.

Fix a good price and name it. If a client seems to falter, you can adjust it by adding, "but Wordsworth here qualifies for a scholarship" and naming a lower price.

DEAR MISS MANNERS:

While performing a construction job for a customer, the customer offered a bonus if we could meet certain criteria by a given date. We completed all the requirements by the appointed time and submitted the final invoice and of course we did not include the promised bonus in the invoice.

At the conclusion of the project, the customer made no mention of the bonus. The promised bonus was significant but I don't know how to remind the customer or know if it would be proper to do so. I do not want to offend our customers, as they have paid us promptly for our work and have been good customers.

GENTLE READER:

If they are good customers, Miss Manners suggests thanking them. That would include saying, "You were kind enough to offer us a bonus, and we were happy to be able to meet your deadline."

DEAR MISS MANNERS:

Is it appropriate for a company who has given out bonuses every year for at least seven years to notify the staff if they do not plan on doing that for this year? I want to know to be prepared, but am afraid that I will appear rude.

GENTLE READER:

What you want to avoid is a "no more gravy train for you folks" tone. But yes, if the employees seem to be counting on their regular bonuses, it is well to warn them.

Miss Manners advises putting it in the form of an apologetic appreciation: "As you all know, we've had a tough year here in spite of your good work. I am sorry to say that bonuses will be impossible, although you certainly deserve them. With your help, I'm sure we'll pull through to better times."

DEAR MISS MANNERS:

As employees of a small manufacturing plant, we are given $25 gift certificates at Christmas from a very expensive department store. The prices for washcloths, bath towels, bathmats are inflated, and clothing, even neckties, are out of sight.

Most people in this plant are single college students, single mothers, or women working to supplement their husbands' Social Security. The highest-paid employee probably makes only slightly more than minimum wage. How do you pay these prices on this kind of wage? Everyone usually has to put money with the certificate in order to get something they can use.

How can we impress upon the bosses to give certificates from some other store where the money would go farther? We realize we're not supposed to look a gift horse in the mouth, but the situation seems ridiculous when some employees are having such a hard time making ends meet, and some are usually laid off for two or three months about a month before Christmas.

GENTLE READER:

It distresses Miss Manners that even you do not see the real problem here. The real problem is that you need a workhorse, instead of a gift horse.

Don't even suggest a gift certificate from another store. It is only too likely that other employees could find another store inappropriate for other reasons. And at best, it is inconvenient to have commercial restrictions fettering what should be your annual bonus, to use as you will.

Send a joint memo from all departments affected (no individual names necessary, lest they be mistakenly targeted as troublemakers) thanking your employer but calling attention to the problem and asking for straight bonuses. That this will also call subtle attention to the fact that luxury-loving bosses have little picture of what it is to live on a meager wage scale is not your fault.

DEAR MISS MANNERS:

Hello, what is the etiquette on tipping the owner of a business?

GENTLE READER:

According to whom?

Those of us who actually know etiquette can tell you authoritatively that it is improper to tip the owner of a business. Tipping is done to supplement the inadequate wages of service employees, and should be considered insulting by entrepreneurs.

However, Miss Manners is given to understand there are entrepreneurs who do not mind being insulted when it comes to money. She finds that regrettable.

GETTING MORE

DEAR MISS MANNERS:

I approve expense accounts for a small team at my company. I suspect one of my team is padding her expense reports with meals with friends, taxi rides, and personal cell phone calls that she says were for business. She follows company rules for filing, claiming these are business expenses, but her reports are routinely higher than her peers by $50 to $100 or more. Is there a subtle way to check that her expenditures are genuine?

GENTLE READER:

Receipts?

The last Miss Manners checked, it was a legitimate business practice for those checking expense accounts to request explanations and documentation. All one has to do to avoid casting rude (which is to say, premature) aspersions on an individual's honesty is to maintain a neutral tone and claim that spot-checking is routine.

Okay, you want a subtle way. Tell her that you want to go over her accounts in detail because the fact that they are higher than anyone else's makes you worry that the other employees are not claiming the expenses to which they are entitled.

DEAR MISS MANNERS:

Is it proper to require all to contribute a required amount for a Christmas gift for the boss?

In past years, Christmas bonuses were common, but in the last two years, boxes of candy or popcorn have been the gifts to staff members.

Much to our surprise, this year there was no gift, not even a card. But everyone was required to contribute a certain amount of money for gifts for our two bosses.

GENTLE READER:

What you are describing is known as a kickback. While the case can be made that it is an ancient custom, Miss Manners does not believe that it is a savory one.

She does appreciate its being a difficult offer to refuse, but she wishes you had come to her before you succumbed. You should have told the collector that you were taking care of holiday wishes to your boss. You would then write him a group letter wishing him the best and saying how glad you all are to be working for him.

GETTING AWAY

DEAR MISS MANNERS:

Among close friends, it is common knowledge that my husband owns a fair amount of stock in the company he works for. Recently the stock went up exponentially. This was discussed in various newspapers and television programs and surrounded by much fanfare.

Now some friends, acquaintances, and even those we have just met ask pointed questions, such as "Are you millionaires?", "How rich are you now?", and the like. Some friends have phoned or written to congratulate us, and we thank them. But how do we respond to awkward questions regarding our finances?

GENTLE READER:

Smoothly, rather than awkwardly. You don't get flustered, you don't seem to be avoiding the question (although you are)—you simply reply, "Well, it certainly was a nice little surprise."

The important part, Miss Manners cautions you, is the delivery. You need an amused smile that says, "I can understand that that would seem like a lot of money to you." Whether this implies that you received much less than is assumed, or that you already had enough to make this amount less important to you than they imagine, doesn't matter.

DEAR MISS MANNERS:

My father-in-law has always disliked me and even told his daughter that I was wrong for her. Heck, he didn't even attend our wedding. But now that my company's going public, he's demanding friends-and-family shares. He's never been much of a friend or family, but I'm getting pressure from my wife to slip him a few. What should I do?

GENTLE READER:

You could slip him a few or you could do him a much bigger favor.

Miss Manners notices that your father-in-law has a long-term investment in the theory that you don't belong in his family. The biggest favor you could do him is to give him the chance to say, "You see? Didn't I tell you how selfish he is? He's not interested in the family, he's just out for himself. This isn't about me, you know; it's about you. You're his own wife, and you ask him to do something and what happens? It doesn't make any difference what you say, does it? That's the kind of husband he is. He doesn't care about you, he doesn't care about any of us. I could see that from the beginning . . ." and so on.

DEAR MISS MANNERS:

I recently took a job at a dotcom company and was shocked when my neighbor and several acquaintances asked if I was making a lot of money and if I had received stock options. My mother always taught me that it is rude to ask personal finance questions. How should I respond to them?

GENTLE READER:

By saying, "My mother always taught me that it is rude to discuss my personal finances."

Note that Miss Manners has done some editing here, but she trusts that your mother would approve. Having brought you up properly, your mother surely also told you that it is rude to tell people they are being rude, even when they clearly are.

DEAR MISS MANNERS:

I am a professional artist. I show my work frequently and sell many pieces. However, like many independent artists, I don't make as much money as others in regular, full-time employment. I am very lucky to have a supportive spouse helping to cover the household expenses.

When I tell people I am a full-time artist, they often ask if I make enough money to support myself. I usually answer truthfully, saying no, or not yet, and adding that my spouse helps support me.

However, I fear that answering this way leads people to look upon me as a dilettante or a housewife with a hobby, which I am not—I am a serious professional, building a career. I am aware that how much money I earn is nobody's business and I am not obliged to answer these questions at all. I would much appreciate any suggestions for deflecting them—politely, of course.

GENTLE READER:

"Yes, it's a sure road to easy riches. You should try it."

Part 3

The Long Haul—Off the Job

CHAPTER 10

Off the Premises

That we have become inured to the blurring of the distinction between personal and professional conduct is nowhere more apparent to Miss Manners than in the area of business travel. But she seems to be going it alone.

The sales manager sets off on a trip with her young assistant sales manager. As the assistant lives closer to the airport than the manager, she gives him a ride. As the assistant is wrestling both sets of luggage onto a cart, the manager looks at the departures board only to discover that the flight has been cancelled. With the help of her smartphone, she is able to rebook them and she and her protégée go to different counters to check in for the flight.

Does no one else wonder what rules motivated such behavior? The ride to the airport was no doubt kind as well as practical, the act of a mentor. And it saved either the assistant or the company the cost of parking. Assuming that both the manager and her assistant are essentially equally able-bodied, did the assistant carry the luggage because he was the junior business partner, the gentleman, or younger? Did the boss reschedule the flight because she had greater authority or a faster telephone? Or was she acting as the host?

And if any of these sets of manners—all of which carry reciprocal but uneven obligations—applied, why the separate check-in?

Miss Manners is surprised that the assistant who is so shrill in his objection to fetching coffee has nothing to say about hauling luggage, and equally amazed that the boss who is so vocal on the subject of assistants who cannot take the initiative is happy to act as travel agent. The fact is that business travel is a world unto itself, although we hope a respectable one. Even on a free night, coworkers often socialize, if only to avoid eating alone.

However, normal rules of business etiquette still apply whenever the activity is an unavoidable component of the trip. There are more comfortable ways to exit a building than throwing everything out the window.

This means that the flight, the cab, the check-in—perhaps even the business breakfast—is no less a business function than the day's meetings, although less formal. If carrying luggage is part of the assistant sales manager's deference to a boss, so be it. If handling the ticketing is a management function, Miss Manners makes no objection. But both should be functions of rank, not of such personal attributes as gender or age. Trouble occurs when participants are left to guess—a situation one would think businesses, who seem mad for endless personnel policies, could easily remedy.

That personal time will be limited during business travel does not mean it disappears. Miss Manners objects to cavalier assumptions by the boss that he has control over his employees' time off, and she redoubles her objections when it comes to business travel. Taking everyone out to dinner in an unfamiliar city may be a kind gesture, but it is all the more important to respect employees'—and bosses' and coworkers'—privacy when it is so scarce. The best way to deal with an unwanted roommate is not to borrow his toothbrush.

DEAR MISS MANNERS:

I have occasion to travel frequently on business with a young man thirty years my junior. We have a symbiotic relationship, I needing him to perform my duties and he needing me for his subsistence. He does his job extremely well—if one is resigned to ignore his breach of the amenities.

I am aware of the generation gap in regards to etiquette, but if his lack of observance of basic manners were, by chance, observed by others, it would make him appear boorish and uncivil. To me, it shows unforgivable disrespect.

For example, he always struts ahead at airports without glancing back to see if I'm following or lost in the crowd; he never holds a door for me but always walks into a room with me bringing up the rear; he never stands when I or any other lady approaches the table; he always helps himself to salt and pepper, butter, etc., at the dinner table and passes it to me only if asked. In every social situation he regards me as a convenient adjunct, not a woman requiring at least a minimum of consideration.

I believe he behaves in this manner out of ignorance, not with a deliberate desire to be offensive. In every other respect, he is an entertaining, charming, and capable young man who does his job extremely well.

I hasten to add that this is purely a business association, not to be confused with the current affinity of older women for "boy toys." I am eager to maintain a civil association.

GENTLE READER:

In that case, why are you complaining that he doesn't offer you deference as a woman? Why aren't you complaining that he doesn't offer you deference as his boss? And why aren't you directing that complaint to him?

Were you toying with the young gentleman personally, Miss Manners could understand a reluctance to demand more attention from him. Romantic reform is a delicate matter under any circumstances, and it is not made easier when there is a difference of generations, giving the younger person the opportunity to claim erroneously that the etiquette rules you cite have been canceled.

But while instructions to employees should be given politely, they should be neither unexpected nor resented. Tell him how well you think he does his job otherwise, but that you wish him to maintain a stance of respectful attention, and supply him with specific instructions. If he pouts and pleads "Why can't you love me the way I am?" he is the one who is mistaken about the nature of the relationship.

It Isn't Supposed to Be Vacation

DEAR MISS MANNERS:

My boyfriend recently went to Hawaii on a business trip that I could not accompany him on. He left on Thursday and will get back Tuesday, and he only called me once and sent texts 2–3 times only to say he was going to sleep now.

He gave me a quick rundown of his itinerary, so I know he was busy with clients, a show (work related) and/or physical labor at the warehouse. But I suppose I was hoping for more . . . yes, I wanted him to call me, in spite of the time difference.

He only told me that he loved me when I asked him if everything was okay and if he loved me. I love this man very much, but I am beginning to think that "he is not into me" anymore. What do you think?

GENTLE READER:

That it is no fun to listen to whines for more attention when in the middle of a short, hectic, and tiring business trip.

Whether the gentleman harbored that thought, or how he feels about you, Miss Manners has no way of knowing. She only hopes that you will welcome him home in a spirit that says you are glad to have him back, rather than that you are concerned about him only in relation to yourself.

At Least Not All of It

DEAR MISS MANNERS:

Is it ethically correct to attach personal vacations on the ends of business travel arrangements?

As a young adult entering the workforce, I will be traveling to Europe this spring (for the first time!) and would love to append some time at the end of my business to visit a friend. As the travel costs are being paid by my employer, I seem to find myself in a morally gray area.

My mother tells me I shouldn't mix business with pleasure. Everyone else says it is not a problem, and "everyone" does it. Clearly "everyone doing it" is not a justification for taking advantage of this "opportunity." However, the extra costs would be paid for by me, and would cost my employer nothing.

GENTLE READER:

Allow Miss Manners to begin by saying that she admires your moral fastidiousness, and hopes that your employers appreciate you. Apparently they do, or you wouldn't be entering the workforce with a job that features business trips abroad.

Then she feels obliged to establish her own ethical level, as opposed to the one on which one finds those morally careless folks known as "everyone." Miss Manners is possibly the only person in the universe who believes that it is wrong to take home a paper clip supply from the office or unused toiletries from hotel rooms. Also, you may have noticed that she supports the principle of separating business from pleasure.

While some businesses object to the practice, Miss Manners cannot fathom what could be wrong with taking advantage of business travel to have one's holiday abroad afterward. It seems a fitting compensation for the fact that travel, however glamorous, makes inroads on one's private time, if for no other reason than because one cannot go home at night. As doing this will require consulting your supervisors in order to schedule your vacation and change your travel dates, you will have an ample opportunity to discuss any objection they might raise that Miss Manners has unaccountably overlooked.

Alarming Roommates

DEAR MISS MANNERS:

Twice a year I share a hotel room with another woman in our company for 3–4 nights. I think we should be thoughtful to one another when it comes to setting an early wake-up call.

She likes to rise extremely early to exercise, therefore waking me up 1–2 hours before I really want to be awakened. I am not exactly a light sleeper, but I cannot go back to a slumber after the alarm sounds.

She says everyone is free to sound the alarm whenever they please. I think she is being rude. What do you think? I need more sleep to function well at these conferences we attend. It makes the day really long when the alarm sounds at 5:30 a.m.

GENTLE READER:

Really? Your roommate declares that all people, presumably including everyone in her hotel room, are free to sound the alarm whenever they please?

No, let's not go there. Miss Manners does not suggest that you follow the purported etiquette rules of someone who does not recognize any need for considering the well-being of others.

It is time for you to go to the person who handles arrangements at your company and request another roommate. Your point should be that the behavior of your present roommate prevents you from getting the rest that you need to be in top working form.

DEAR MISS MANNERS:

For my company's management retreat in Miami next month, we're assigned rooms (with twin beds) to share with colleagues of the same sex. I am not relishing the idea of a forced sleepover with a coworker. What does Miss Manners make of this practice?

GENTLE READER:

She doesn't think much of the practice of retreats, even if they have improved somewhat since the days when employees were bullied to say damaging things about themselves and their colleagues. They still disrupt people's private lives and foist overtime on them as if it were a treat.

But since you object only to the rooming arrangements, Miss Manners will cut off what would otherwise have been a full-blown attack on a popular custom. What she thinks of the practice of assigning double rooms is that it is cheaper than providing single ones. To get your own room, you must convince the planner that it would cost less, in time and effort, if not in money. Try "I work through the night, and a roommate would complain to you about the light and noise." In the therapeutic-style retreat, smart employees would confess only to being overly devoted to work.

What Did You Bring Me?

DEAR MISS MANNERS:

I am the director at a small museum with a staff of 8. Many times when I travel (which is not too often), I bring my team a little something, mostly from museum shops in the places I've visited. There is one staff member in particular that I greatly dislike, and have no respect for. I have always included him in my gifts (I bring the same item for everyone) in spite of my dislike for him, because I think that is the proper etiquette for a boss.

However, this last holiday, I bought a very nice gift for everyone, except for him—I felt it would have been very hypocritical for me to do so, since at this point I cannot even tolerate his presence. Did I do the right thing? Is one supposed to give gifts out of "professional obligation" and not fondness and gratitude, which I feel toward everyone else in my team?

GENTLE READER:

The professional obligation you refer to is one with which Miss Manners is not familiar. She would ask if you also consider it a supervisory responsibility to buy your employees cake on their birthdays did she not, unfortunately, already know the answer.

You have stumbled on yet another of the many difficulties that crop up as a result of mixing the personal with the professional, but one that you had apparently avoided so long as the gifts were "a little something." Your motivation was, as you say, to show appreciation for your employees. Let us assume that it was taken in that spirit, and not as a reminder that you were in sunny Aruba while they were shuffling to work through the snow. But to use such a gesture to snub a disliked employee is unseemly. In future, it would be simpler if, on your business trips, you confined your activities to business matters.

What Can I Bring You?

DEAR MISS MANNERS:

My department at work is holding a two-day meeting, which representatives from other company facilities out of state will be attending. One of our executives has offered to host a barbecue at his home to show hospitality to our out-of-state coworkers. Typically the company would pay for all meals for the traveling employees, so in a way it is a business dinner, but I think it's a lovely gesture on the executive's part to invite everyone to his home. I am a "local" but I'll be attending the barbecue.

Is it appropriate in this situation for me to bring a host/hostess gift for this gentleman and his wife? If so, what would be a proper gift? I don't drink and know very little about wine and other alcoholic beverages, so I'd prefer to give something different.

GENTLE READER:

Indeed, the executive should be thanked by the company, and if you were its owner, you would have the problem of thinking of a suitably graceful way to do so. But as an individual, your bringing a so-called hostess gift will not only annoy your colleagues who didn't, but will suggest that you are there as his personal guest—or at least, as you are local, a potential new friend.

However, Miss Manners is far from discouraging you from distinguishing yourself with your generosity. What would be really charming for you to do would be to tell the executive that you, as a local, are in a position to help him out by doing any chores related to the party, including just standing by at the time to take care of any small problem that might arise. Putting out fires, so to speak, as it is a barbecue. Now that is the sort of thing that inspires warmth in any host.

CHAPTER 11

What Can You Do For Me?

Come Attend an Art Opening at
the Becky Sharp Gallery and Share
A GLASS OF CHAMPAGNE WITH MR. SEDLEY,
the Inventor of the Doodle Drive, and
Other IT Professionals Like Yourself.

Miss Manners now understands that IT is an acronym referring to things computer-related, rather than a grouping of emphatic Clara Bow fans. The invitation has explained that this is a Once in a Lifetime Opportunity, full of OPPORTUNITY and PROMISE. And she recognizes that everyone involved agrees with this latter statement, even if the capitalization is beginning to give her a headache.

She just does not understand why. By donating his time to the Gallery—now Miss Manners is doing it (over-capitalizing; she was already donating, though perhaps not to the gallery in question)—Mr. Sedley (who is grammatically credited with having invented Professionals Like Yourself) is to be commended. And as a charitable institution, the gallery is understandably in it to make a buck.

But what exactly are the attendees thinking? That it would be entertaining to get some work done if one is forced to take an evening away from the office? That new professional avenues will be opened up by drinking in front of a business bigwig? That the champagne will be any good?

Surely not.

As Americans, we invert the traditional British disdain of "trade." We save our disdain for those who do not work, including those who have no need of doing so. We have even taught them a thing or two about the dignity of labor, especially when faced with ruinous inheritance taxes. However, we could use a bit more restraint and grace at the necessary precursor, namely making personal contacts that may lead to gainful employment.

Computer professionals are in one of the few occupations in which the Internet has, to a limited extent, succeeded in depersonalizing the hiring process. In almost every other field, Knowing Someone—it really is a disease, isn't it?—confers a distinct advantage, whether that means being the offspring of the owner, or, more likely, having a mentor or well-placed friend interested in your succeeding, or at least in your getting off the dole—or the couch.

Networking is one of the few areas in which the personal and the professional overlap with Miss Manners' blessing, albeit a limited one. One would wish that everyone had the opportunity to benefit from, and be grateful to, a teacher, friend, or colleague who can provide professional assistance, if not a fond relative looking to hand over the business.

But even then, and emphatically when approaching an acquaintance, the appeal must be decently separated from the social connection. Being cornered at a party to be asked, "Can you get me into your firm?" is a social menace. But it is flattering to hear, "I am graduating this June and am so interested in what you do. Could I invite you to lunch to ask for some advice on how to pursue this?" The chance to speak about the topic without the distractions of a social setting shows a seriousness of purpose that can only impress.

Most importantly, you must have signs that the person in question is a willing, even eager, participant. Do you want a reference that takes the form, "Would you please, please, please do an informational interview with my friend's son, so he'll stop cornering me at parties"? Or, from someone aware of the Freedom of Information Act, "I've never worked with him, but I can assure you that he is a fine fellow who will enliven your office, because he is a great practical joker"?

Hoping to Advance

DEAR MISS MANNERS:

The "social" hour before business-related meetings, luncheons, and dinners is tailor-made for making contacts, finding out about job openings and keeping tabs on the competition.

But this prime networking situation is often nearly wasted because I get stuck talking to one or two people. While they may be great to get to know in a purely social situation, they may offer little to nothing in terms of the business-type conversation/information I am looking for. What is the most polite way to excuse myself so that I can identify and talk to others of more interest to me?

GENTLE READER:

The cocktail party social climber who always looks beyond a current conversation partner in the hope of finding someone more interesting has given this sort of mixing a bad name. So have people who move on after claiming that they must go get drinks or take telephone calls, and are clearly observed to be doing no such thing.

But Miss Manners assures you that stand-up gatherings, even social ones, were designed specifically so that many people may meet and talk in a short time, as you wish to do. Thus, leaving one person to find another is not an intrinsically rude concept.

The trick is to provide a strong conclusion to the conversation, rather than a weak excuse. Delivered heartily, "I'm so glad I had a chance to meet you—this was fascinating, and I hope to see you again," is charming. You still depart, but not with that sneaking look that always accompanies a murmured version of, "Whoops, I think I hear my mother calling me."

DEAR MISS MANNERS:

How should a professional deal with clients who do not have good manners? I am an attorney. Since 1998, I have represented a company in a litigation matter that is still ongoing. At times, I have had almost daily dealings with Ms. X, my client contact; at other times, we can go for several weeks without contact.

Recently, I read that this same client was sued in a matter unrelated to the litigation I am handling, but in an area where I have extensive experience for other clients. I called Ms. X and left a detailed voicemail asking her to call me, at her convenience, so that we could discuss the matter. The next day, I followed up with an email in which I listed my qualifications in this area and the qualifications of other members of my firm to assist the client in this new matter.

I also asked her to let me know, one way or the other, whether this was something she would be interested in discussing with me. After three more days, I followed up with a phone call and left a message with Ms. X's secretary asking Ms. X to call me about the new litigation.

A couple of weeks later, I called Ms. X to discuss a matter in the case I am handling. When we had finished discussing that matter, she quickly said, "Oh, on that other matter, sorry I never got back to you, I've just been swamped."

In response, all I said was, "Have you been too busy to retain counsel?" She then told me that she had retained other counsel.

One of my partners told me that my response was inappropriate, that I should have said something like, "Oh, that's okay" in response to her statement that she was very busy. I obviously disagree, since I do not think it was okay.

Granted, all of my calls were part of an effort to persuade Ms. X to hire me to handle the new litigation, but I still think it is rude to ignore professional phone calls, and that she should have returned my call even if it was simply to thank me for my interest and then inform me that the company had already retained other counsel. Moreover, I do not consider her uttering the word "sorry" to be an apology, so I don't think I was under any compulsion to accept this non-heartfelt apology.

Was I wrong? Although I do not think it matters, Ms. X has never informed me that she was displeased with how I have handled the ongoing litigation. My position is that, even if she was displeased, she still should have had the common courtesy to return my phone calls.

GENTLE READER:

Miss Manners trusts that you are one of those rare lawyers who immediately returns all telephone calls and would never dream of keeping a client waiting. But are you also so meticulous in responding to solicitations to purchase something?

In such cases, the understanding is that the target responds if interested. If you use an existing social or business relationship to embarrass the person into giving your offer special consideration, you have to allow for the fact that the person will, in fact, be embarrassed.

Sometimes such a person is embarrassed into saying yes when the answer would otherwise have been no; other times, as is the case here, the target simply hides. Your continuing to pursue the matter when the client was obviously not interested sounds to Miss Manners remarkably like hounding.

DEAR MISS MANNERS:

When I was a technical consultant, I was always happy to offer free advice to family or friends, making it clear that it was "off the cuff" and did not take advantage of all the firm's resources that I could enlist for a paying client.

My new business involves wholesale chocolate products. I would like to offer a courtesy price to family and friends, but what is an appropriate discount? 10 percent? Wholesale price? My cost? Should I dodge the sale and send them to a retailer?

Promotion of a new product is good business, and surely my friends would tell their friends. But my business is brand-new, my promotional allowance is limited, and I can give away free only a very small amount. I don't want to be a Scrooge, but I don't want to be a sap, either.

GENTLE READER:

Free chocolates? Where?

Miss Manners didn't mean to get overexcited, and it is not a pretty reaction. Her point is that you don't want to provoke it in your friends.

Rather than talking to their own friends about this treat, the recipients of your largesse are more likely to be talking constantly to you: "I need an extra box to send to a friend of mine." "Only 10 percent off for a friend? Why, I buy in bulk and get things cheaper than that." "They're great; I'm giving a party and I need enough for dessert for about 50 people."

Miss Manners believes you would be far better off to take your allowance of free chocolates home, and serve them to your friends when they are guests, saying, "This is the chocolate from the company I represent—tell me what you think of it."

DEAR MISS MANNERS:

I had a sporadic but mutually beneficial professional relationship with someone who was, 25 years ago, a dear college friend (she is a feminist academic, I am in publishing). I forwarded a non-academic job listing in her specialty to her, thinking it possible she might be tempted, but certain that she would know qualified people (students or former coworkers) who would be interested. Her immediate response was one line: "I'm too busy to recruit for you or anybody."

I was astonished—that she would not support the "old girl" network, and that she would take the time to be rude when she could easily have not replied at all. We're both busy working parents. I don't clutter up her mailbox with trivia. I decided not to respond, in case explaining any of this might have been rude. Maybe she was just having a bad day, but this incident has cooled my feelings toward her. Was I "recruiting"? And was this bad?

GENTLE READER:

The issue here is not whether she acceded to your reasonable request. As you point out, she could have politely ignored it, on the grounds that it was a widespread feeler to which only those with something to suggest need respond.

Even less is the issue whether she was having a bad day. Feeling surly is no excuse for acting surly, Miss Manners reminds you. Neither is feeling aggrieved, so, as you realize, you cannot snap back with an accusation of rudeness. But you can snap back with a cold apology: "I'm so sorry to have imposed on you. I promise it won't happen again."

Having to Retreat

DEAR MISS MANNERS:

A friend wants a job at my company and asked if I'd give her an "in." While she's a great personal friend, I don't think she's qualified for the position, and she has a spotty employment history. I don't want to hurt her feelings. Do I turn her off the company or let her go through the interview process and let the company decide? If my employer asks for my opinion, I can't in good conscience give a positive one. If I brush my friend off with a vague excuse, I know she'll dig and dig.

GENTLE READER:

You certainly don't want to offer a frank excuse, which would be, "Don't even try, they only want top-notch people like me."

Miss Manners is aware that people often dig when they encounter vague excuses, but they have to stop digging when they hit rock. To your friend, you say, "I can introduce you if you want, but frankly, I think you'd be making a big mistake. I know you and I know them, and even though it works for me, I know it's wrong for you, and they're not going to appreciate what you have to offer." To your employer, you say, "I can only tell you she's a great friend."

DEAR MISS MANNERS:

A former subcontractor of mine has asked me to be a reference on a job application. I agreed to do so, but am applying for the same position. I have not informed the subcontractor of my application. Should I inform the subcontractor? Should I withdraw myself as a reference?

GENTLE READER:

If you did not recuse yourself, what would you write? An enthusiastic endorsement that might eclipse your own application? A tempered one that would smack of sabotaging a rival?

And if you get the job without having told the subcontractor that you were applying, might he not assume that his request inspired you to grab the job for yourself?

Courtesy alone should prompt you to tell the subcontractor that although you think highly of him, it would be a conflict of interest for you, as you had already applied for the job. Miss Manners is always happy to bolster etiquette requirements with a glimpse into the consequences of violating them.

DEAR MISS MANNERS:

I am in a position to outsource work, and with all the layoffs, family and friends are coming at me in droves looking for any crumbs. They make me feel guilty when I say, "There is no work to be had" (not true) or "I keep personal and professional matters separate" (sort of true).

The real reason? I don't expect high-caliber work from people who do it only for the money. Is there a way to deny these would-be contractors, consultants, and freelancers without looking coldhearted?

GENTLE READER:

What other reaction could you possibly expect to the announcement that you are not willing to help out friends in need when it is easily within your power? Gratitude?

Mind you, Miss Manners is not suggesting that you do this. Only that you take their point of view. You could say, "I'm worried about conflict of interest. It could backfire if I recommend my friends—they're going to assume you wouldn't be able to get the job otherwise. You're better off trying another route and not letting on that you know me."

DEAR MISS MANNERS:

With all the troubles in the economy, I have a number of friends who are unemployed, some for a great deal of time. I also have friends who are still very successfully employed, even supervising large numbers of people and in a position to influence hiring. I am often being asked by friends seeking employment to mention this fact to friends who might be in a position to hire.

I'm always happy to help, but I get a very funny feeling about going to have lunch with a friend and then listing a few people who've asked me to mention they're looking for work. On the other hand, I'm told that this is basic networking and it's perfectly acceptable to do on a friend's behalf. So I'm not sure which way to dodge. Am I being foolish to worry about this? What's the best way to be helpful to my friends?

GENTLE READER:

Secondhand networking is actually a great deal more tactful than the firsthand kind, where the candidate and the target are both bound to be embarrassed if it turns out not to be a good match.

All you need do is to alert your hiring friends that you know some good people in case they are looking, and let them take it up or drop it. Miss Manners only cautions you not to mislead either side—the prospective employer by claiming merits for which you cannot vouch, or the prospective employees by predicting success for which you cannot vouch. Although this is really a matter of ethics, it would create etiquette problems.

Following Through

DEAR MISS MANNERS:

Prior to my moving to a new job, I wrote letters of appreciation to some of my clients, bidding farewell and asking for letters of reference if they were pleased with my services. I enclosed stamped, self-addressed envelopes.

Some have called with well-wishes and promises of letters. As these letters come in, should I then write thank-yous? I want to balance appreciation with closure, moving on. Your advice is appreciated.

GENTLE READER:

So is your interest in thank-you letters. Miss Manners so rarely has the opportunity of warning people not to overdo them.

The danger here, as you have guessed, is their thinking you are not moving on, and that they will therefore be expected to do yet another favor. Therefore a quick note saying that the letter was of great help is better than a saga that itself seems to require acknowledgment.

DEAR MISS MANNERS:

I am planning on going into business, having become interested in this particular industry through a local proprietor of the same goods and services. He was always friendly and helpful and I enjoyed shopping there.

What is proper for me to do in regard to the relationship with this person? I'm worried he'll feel betrayed after he helped me so often.

GENTLE READER:

The proper thing to do is to define the relationship. Miss Manners assures you that if you are the first to tell him of your plans, and you thank him for being your mentor and role model, he will have to consider you as his grateful protégé rather than as his competitor.

DEAR MISS MANNERS:

When I knew I was about to lose my job, I mentioned my availability to a few people in case they knew of anyone hiring software engineers. It turned out that one of them was the sister-in-law of the high-profile CEO of a large software company. She asked me to bring my résumé the next time we met.

I had expected that she would pass the résumé on to her brother-in-law, but when I gave it to her, she looked confused and told me to mail it to him at work, as she wouldn't be seeing him. I asked if she knew of an email address I could send it to, and she said she only had his personal address and didn't feel comfortable giving it out.

She's a motherly kind of woman who is new to the Internet, and probably believes that you need to send a paper résumé to be taken seriously, which isn't the case in the software industry.

I appreciate the referral, but you can't just mail a résumé to the CEO of a large company without any sort of introduction. I did send it, in case he was waiting for it, but he never replied. I doubt that it even made it past his mail screener, who wouldn't have recognized this woman's name when I mentioned her in the cover letter.

How could I have turned the situation around? Should I have asked her to email it for me? Or asked if she'd let him know to expect my letter? How could I have let her know that the referral was useless without an introduction, without sounding ungracious?

GENTLE READER:

The lady already knew it was useless, Miss Manners is sorry to have to tell you. Between the time she made her impulsive offer and the next time she saw you, she found out that her brother-in-law was not interested in the referral—or perhaps she simply reflected that he would not be.

This need not be a reflection on you. If you were a CEO, it is possible that you would approve a personnel policy that failed to give preference to your motherly sister-in-law's acquaintances.

Networking has its limits. It is all very well to make it known that you are job-hunting, but you cannot dictate the type of help to be given.

CHAPTER 12

Party Time

A significant change has taken place in the traditional office party, Miss Manners observes. She only hopes that she isn't also being observed sneaking out early. It's not that she wants to escape the folks at work. It's just that she would have to put in too many more hours at (or in) the punch bowl before she went along with such merry ideas as how much fun it would be to roast the boss.

The office party comes in many forms, the Christmas party being the grandfather of them all. Traditionalists will be glad to hear that the change Miss Manners observed has not affected its most notable feature. It still provides every employee with an equal opportunity to obliterate a promising career in one carefree moment. That aspect has even been professionalized. The office flirt need not worry the next day about being avoided—the thing to worry about is being sued. The tipsy cut-up will no longer face merciless teasing—it will be merciless counseling.

But the office party was always hazardous for anybody who thought that the key word in the term was "party" and not "office." Encouraged to abandon the prudence that sensible people exercise while pursing their livelihoods, a few otherwise model workers managed to commit professional suicide by being unfortunately funny or frank. Miss Manners thinks it fairer to get those perils out into the open than to let the imprudent behave as if they were among friends who regard them with fond tolerance—and later be slapped with the professional consequences.

The innovation has to do with the basic terms of the party. Office parties were always given by bosses for their employees. The idea was to foster good will and lift morale by offering the workers a treat.

Some bosses actually stood at the door, shook their employees' hands, and told them how much their work was appreciated. Some led singing or dancing. Some gave out presents or prizes that everyone politely pretended not to notice had arrived at the office as Christmas presents from other businesses. Some made total fools of themselves.

But whatever hostly duties each may have done or omitted, and with however much or little charm, it was the bosses who gave those office parties. They planned them and they paid for them, even if that meant, as it always did, that they assigned the planning to a subordinate to perform during working hours and charged the expense to the business. In the world of commerce, this passes for generosity.

At any rate, the employees were the guests. The party was given for their benefit. Now, however, it is more likely that all employees will be assigned to set up the decorations, bring the food and pay for their own drinks—to be, in other words, their own hosts. Instead of receiving a turkey or some other such personally chosen tribute from the boss, the employees may be asked to contribute to buy the boss a present.

Something is very wrong here, Miss Manners can't help noticing. The reversal may have started innocently enough, in a time of financial hardship for the business. Told that the expense of a party could no longer be justified, workers—naturally reluctant to strain budgets that might no longer have been able to justify their salaries, either—sometimes decided to pitch in.

Spirited and generous as that may have been, it set a bad precedent. The bosses seized on this change as a tremendous improvement. Although the concept of entertaining clients at the business's expense survived hard times, that of entertaining employees at the business's expense, even once a year, did not.

Soon not only holiday parties for the workers but celebrations of their promotions and retirements became cooperative ventures. The boss still wanted to preside—just not to participate in the responsibilities and expenses.

The truth is that bosses were never great hosts, although they may have been lavish ones. By nature, they are used to bossing people around, so the old office party was never quite as voluntary a treat as it should have been. Pressure to participate was always there, although it is particularly unseemly under the new circumstances.

Miss Manners has never been enthusiastic about office parties because of the dangers inherent in them, and has lobbied to replace them with such genuine workplace treats as bonuses and time off. But she is horrified to find that, instead, they are being turned upside down. Assigning extra work and extracting tributes is not her idea of a holiday treat.

Do We Have to Invite *Them*?

DEAR MISS MANNERS:

Each year, the employees arrange a party at the local center of the very large international company where my husband works. Volunteers do the organizing, and tickets are sold during business hours.

It has been suggested that most employees would be more comfortable if the management/supervisors did not attend. The company in no way contributes, either financially or by providing the place, etc., but since tickets are sold at the office, I can see no way to exclude certain individuals without being rude. My husband feels that it's okay to for employees to make it an "Hourly Paid Employee Party" since they're paying for it.

GENTLE READER:

Do the executives of this company have any functions for the top level only, without feeling obliged to include the lower-ranking employees? Do they even agonize over whether it is necessary to do so?

Miss Manners rather suspects that inclusiveness is not always the rule; businesses are not social circles, where everyone is equal. She sees nothing wrong in the employees politely defining their own party so that it is clear that their bosses are not included. She can well imagine that the employees would have a jollier, not to mention safer, party by themselves.

DEAR MISS MANNERS:

My boss sent out an invitation to a party he is throwing and only invited 13 people out of 31. He now wants to send a memo to everyone letting them know he is having this party and is unable to invite everyone. Should this be done?

GENTLE READER:

Does he hope to downsize the office without paying severance?

People do not react well to being told, "Ha, ha, I'm having a party and you're not invited!" which is why kindergarteners are so fond of doing it. If you are in a position to influence your boss, Miss Manners suggests telling him to say he is having a retreat for a third of the office, and is excusing the others.

Wallflowers

DEAR MISS MANNERS:

At my office, many employees in my group have worked together for a long time, socialize together outside the office, and often plan group lunches. Unfortunately, they tend to do these things without regard for the personal feelings of anyone else.

Many times when I am sitting in someone's office discussing a work project, others will come in and say, "Who besides you is coming to lunch?," discuss the arrangements, and walk out without asking me if I want to go, too.

Luckily for me, I do not have much in common with these people, have my own friends outside of work, and do not strive to become part of their clique. However, I still feel some hurt in the face of their absolutely bad manners.

I had a big party last year and only invited one person from my office—but, Miss Manners, I did not discuss the party with that person in front of everyone else! It would have been bad manners, and have even obligated me to invite people I didn't care to have come.

How should I behave while I am trapped in the same room with these people who are being so rude? What I now do is try to become invisible—sit very still and stare at the bookshelf or out the window.

Often someone will say to me a little later, "Are you coming with us to lunch?" Am I supposed to consider this an invitation? I hesitate to say, "I wasn't invited." What I tend to do is try to save my pride, and avoid making people angry, by pleading lack of funds.

GENTLE READER:

Miss Manners can see that you are working yourself up into a really good sulk. But it is over nothing. Office lunch is not the social equivalent of a private party, and the social rule you rightly observe about not discussing plans in front of the uninvited does not apply.

Arrangements are made casually; you will wait in vain for even those anxious to know you to request the pleasure of your company. "Are you coming with us?" is breezy but not rude. People can also politely propose themselves—"Is this a working lunch, or could I join you?"

If you genuinely don't want to go, you need only say a cheerful "Have fun" as they leave. But those comments about cliques and having nothing in common sound to Miss Manners like self-pity, which is inappropriate.

DEAR MISS MANNERS:

For someone looking for a permanent job, starting as a temporary is a good way to find out what a company is really like on the inside. When I accept an assignment as a temporary secretarial employee, I go with the attitude that I am a member of that firm's workforce for the length of time I am there.

However, only too often, "temps" are treated in a demeaning manner, as though they are ignorant and unskilled. (In actuality, most are highly skilled, since they must undergo rigorous testing by the temporary services agency.)

Can you imagine the put-down feeling when there is a birthday cake and celebration for one of the permanent employees and everyone is invited except the "temp"? Can you imagine a Christmas party where every single employee rose, as though on cue, and went to the party, leaving the "temp"—myself—sitting alone in the room?

Every firm is not, of course, this rude. It is a pleasure to work at a place where you are introduced to the other people, shown the coffee room and restroom, told that you can take breaks just like the other employees. It is even pleasanter when someone there invites you to lunch.

GENTLE READER:

Miss Manners is happy to assist you in championing the cause of politeness toward those essential workers who pass through an office in time of extra need. Kindness and appreciation are due them both as workers and as newcomers—perhaps also, as you suggest, as prospective staff.

Introductions and office courtesies should be a matter of course. In fact, these should not be left to chance, but should be an assigned task. But she hopes you will not classify her with the callous when she inquires whether the temporary worker may not be exactly the person to cover while the employees celebrate a birthday or participate in other quasi-social activities based on their long-term ties to one another.

Mind you, Miss Manners has always been against partying in the office. Her idea of an office party is the announcement that everyone can take the rest of the day off, with those who choose to celebrate together gathering off the premises, and others perhaps preferring to go home. Birthday cakes and showers, with their inevitably burdensome collections of money for those whom one may not voluntarily choose as friends, seem to her to be oppressive. Again, those who happen to like one another personally ought to pursue their social relations after hours.

However, these occasions are an ongoing part of a pseudo-social life in which those passing through cannot fully participate. They should of course be offered refreshment, but expect neither to take a full part nor to contribute to the office collections supporting these activities.

Party Pooping

DEAR MISS MANNERS:

While we understand that there may be some morale benefits to recognition at the workplace of events in the personal lives of the staff, we are uncomfortable with the practice because:

1. It is difficult to determine which events (e.g., birth, death, marriage, moves) to recognize.
2. One can miss someone or give the appearance of missing someone who may have expressly declined to be recognized in the workplace.
3. Some staff are uncomfortable being included in a group expression.
4. The number of these events can become very large.

Is there a polite response when someone has plunged ahead and sent flowers or a card on behalf of all the staff, and one or more staff do not wish to participate? Is it not appropriate for individual staff to express their feelings as they feel appropriate? In short, can you tell us when group expression is fitting?

GENTLE READER:

If one of your employees gets born in the office, everybody should definitely notice. Otherwise, Miss Manners is for cutting back from current practice, which vastly overdoes the celebrations to the point of being a constant burden.

When an employee gets married or has a child, that person's supervisor should send a letter of congratulation. A card or note signed by everyone who works with that person would also be nice, and there would have to be an awfully good reason (better than discomfort) for refusing to sign one. This is a minimal expression of good will, and Miss Manners doesn't quite see how it could be considered much of a burden.

But showers and presents are a burden, and visits should not be mandated. They are for individual employees who have become friendly with that person to do on their own as would any other friend, who would consider it a pleasure, rather than a chore. Performing acts of intimate friendship is not a job requirement, at least not in respectable employment.

Office milestones, notably retirement, are different; they should be marked in the office. The major expression—party, present, or such, not to mention the pension—is up to management, but colleagues should at least do a congratulatory lunch. Transferring, quitting, or being fired (unless it is for making off with the petty—or serious—cash) also call for some kindness from colleagues. Moving, however many milestones one may move, is neither that sort of a major life event nor an office one, so it is noted informally among the employee's friends.

DEAR MISS MANNERS:

This seems to be a simple situation which has escalated beyond belief. Our boss scheduled a bag lunch in her office to watch her vacation videos. Everyone in the office is fond of her, but we resent being told and not asked if we would like to see the videos.

While this individual incident would not bother us, it seems to be a trend. We are scheduled for lunches for every staff person's birthday, even if the person having the birthday does not really want one. Frankly, we would like this to stop, but fear hurting the boss's feelings and thus have her resent us. We know she means well, but we tend to feel uncomfortable.

GENTLE READER:

What this is, is a simple management idea that has escalated beyond belief. Miss Manners is using the word "simple" in the sense of "not very bright."

She is casting no aspersions on your boss, who, as you say, means well. Oh, perhaps just a tiny aspersion. Your boss has bought too heavily and uncritically into the highly prevalent idea that it is good management to treat employees like members of the family.

It's a phony conceit. Your boss didn't take you on vacation with her like a member of the family, did she? Nor do you benefit from other family benefits, such as being valued regardless of personal merit and being treated with increasing respect as you grow old and perhaps less productive.

You all doubtless have real families, and real friends, as well, whom you can see when you feel like it, and not because you have no choice when they summon you.

For that matter, your boss may also find this a strain. She may be relieved if you gently release her from these pseudo-social burdens. Gently means not picking her own birthday or video show to rebel. As the next staff birthday approaches, someone speaking for the whole office should tell the boss confidentially that the honoree is serious about not wanting a celebration, and that the rest of you have been talking about its having gotten out of hand. "You know, we're really very happy working for you, and proud of our professional behavior," that person should conclude.

Payment in Food

DEAR MISS MANNERS:

My company recently finished a big project that required the staff to work long hours. The project made a lot of money for the company, so as a thank-you to us, our manager threw an office party. While I appreciate the gesture, she ordered keg beer and pizza and held it in our dreary meeting room (as if we don't spend enough time here!). She boasted about what an inexpensive bash it was and said we should have next month's party here. Ugh! This seems like a chintzy reward for all our hard work. How do we tell her so?

GENTLE READER:

There is no polite way to tell your hostess thanks for the party, but it sure was chintzy. However, Miss Manners notices that you have a perfect opening to tell your boss that you would like to save her even more money. Point out that as kind as she is to throw parties (actually, Miss Manners thinks that is on a level with rewarding kindergarteners with a little treat for being good, but that's just between us), it would be cheaper to use the money for bonuses so that no work time is lost.

DEAR MISS MANNERS:

Recently, a client of our newspaper, for which I am a reporter, has invited me to lunch.

I am certain this client, who has a four-figure advertising account with us, intends to do some high-grade kibitzing with me regarding sports coverage. I would rather talk business during regular working hours, instead of during a period of the day which is supposed to be a respite from the stress of the workaday world.

I know business-related meals are considered a necessary evil, but I would like some advice on a polite way to tell this client how I feel, without it sounding like a snub. Or should I go ahead and put up with a lunchtime business talk for the sake of good business relations? Please say I shouldn't have to do it.

GENTLE READER:

Miss Manners will certainly say that, but it would be more useful if your editor told the client that you would love to go but that he forbids it. What are editors for?

If this one is reluctant, you might point out that what you have here is a sure no-winner for the newspaper. Once this client has told you how he thinks sports should be covered, do you think for a moment that he won't check the paper every day to see if you followed his instructions? And is he going to be happy if you don't?

In any case, Miss Manners advises you to cultivate a reputation (with outsiders, not editors) for being too busy working to take time out for lunch.

The One You Brung

DEAR MISS MANNERS:

Setting: my husband's company party at a posh banquet hall. Having been with the company for 15 years, he has just been promoted to president and chief operating officer.

One particular female employee has monopolized him for 45 minutes, despite my and others' efforts to be included. After half an hour of music, the first slow dance begins. He has thus far danced with no one. I proceed to approach him, politely excuse the interruption, and ask my husband to dance this very romantic dance. Said employee grabs his arm and proclaims that she has already claimed the dance. Trying to hide my dismay, I hesitantly relinquish him as she takes my husband to the dance floor.

Am I wrong, Miss Manners, or was this employee a little out of line? What would have been an appropriate response on my part? How should my husband have handled this? Was silence on his part just being polite? And if so, was he polite to her by being thoughtless to me?

I feel taken advantage of and hurt, as my husband won't talk about the incident. About 150 people were present. We are 40, and have been married for 15 years. The employee has been an acquaintance, at work functions only, for 8 years and is about 40 also, and had her husband present at the party.

GENTLE READER:

Would your energies be better spent persuading your husband to go into another line of work? Miss Manners doesn't mean to be critical, but a gentleman who finds himself the hapless victim of a tug-of-war before an assemblage of his own employees is not going to be happy as an executive.

Should he decide to stick it out, however, Miss Manners advises you to learn what a company party is before you risk attending another one. Company parties are given, at company expense, for a company objective—raising morale, perhaps, or enabling their employees to establish some sort of camaraderie. (Miss Manners believes these objectives would be better accomplished with raises, but never mind that here.)

They are not opportunities for the CEO's wife to have a romantic dance with her husband. The only reason to put such an exhibition on for the employees would be to squelch rumors that, for instance, the company president was about to run off with the mailroom clerk and the payroll.

Nor are they opportunities for employees to make a pass at the boss, if that is what you are suggesting. But surely the boss should know whether or not that is taking place—he may indeed have asked an employee to dance, as the purpose of the party was collegiality—and be able to handle anything improper.

If not, he is, as Miss Manners worries, in the wrong line of work. But it seems to Miss Manners that you could help the personal side of the question by admitting that you didn't mean to embarrass him in front of the office, but were overcome with your desire to have a romantic dance, and are still hoping that he will take you dancing privately, away from office cares—and personnel.

DEAR MISS MANNERS:

I arrived at my fiancée's office party after the festivities had started, and my fiancée was dancing and having a good time with a fellow male employee. After the dance, she noticed me and started to advance in my direction, but was interrupted by the same or another male employee to dance again.

She never acknowledged me until several dances afterward. By this time, I felt I would like to leave, as I did not know anyone there and felt out of place. She never introduced me to her superiors and bosses or anyone else.

Later, she mentioned that she has to work and cooperate with this group, although she is a secretary and not employed by these fellow workers. Maybe so, but I still believe one has to live a lifetime with one's future husband, which is more important—or at the very least, deserves some respect.

If the situation had been reversed, she would have been upset. Maybe the situation is one reason why so many marriages end in divorce.

GENTLE READER:

This engagement doesn't sound too solid, either. But if you will permit Miss Manners an attempt to salvage it, she may be able to save both of you future unpleasantness.

"You didn't pay any attention to me" is indeed a common marital battle cry, but then, so is "You didn't give me a chance to talk to anyone." What follows is never pretty.

So let us first put aside any speculation about whether your fiancée has cooled toward you, is ashamed of you in front of others, is more interested in her male coworkers than you, and so on. Miss Manners knows that your mind is racing along those lines, but if you have other reasons to suppose that any such thing is the case, you surely would have mentioned it. Then your only etiquette problem in regard to your fiancée would be how to tell her the engagement is over.

It is possible that the lady simply has not yet learned how to behave socially as part of a couple. This is not as obvious as you may think. While it is true that it was rude to ignore you, it would also have been rude to ignore other guests because you were there.

The correct thing to do would have been to bring her dance partner to you and introduce you to him and others there until you had done your part by striking up a conversation. Miss Manners suggests that you explain the problem cheerfully, and look for an opportunity to demonstrate it at a gathering where you are known and your fiancée is not.

If the lady claims a right to be upset then, but dismisses your being upset, Miss Manners will concede that your engagement might not be worth saving.

Present-Pooping

DEAR MISS MANNERS:

I work as an assistant for a large group of people. Last year for Secretaries Day, I was first asked to order my own gift using the company credit card (which could not be done as this is against corporate policy) and then overheard the other employees complaining about chipping in a few dollars for my gift.

I have never been comfortable with the tradition of awarding the secretary with a plant or lunch for just doing their job and do not require this type of reward, especially when it is given ungraciously. How do I let people know, without offending them as I was offended last year, that a gift is not wanted this year?

GENTLE READER:

How do you let these offensive people know that you don't want their offensive gift, without offending them?

Miss Manners is putting that question in her Too Hard basket. To refuse a present is an insult. However, she will suggest a possibility that is more within your area of expertise. Isn't it true that there are circumstances under which a secretary can politely refuse to take on another activity?

You could politely decline a luncheon invitation on the grounds of having more pressing work to do. And you could accept a plant on behalf of the office, rather than for yourself, placing it at some distance from your desk for everyone to enjoy—and requesting that someone who knows how to take care of plants take on that job.

DEAR MISS MANNERS:

Every Christmas at my office, the members of my department have a Secret Santa party, at which we each give a gift to the person whose name we've previously pulled out of a hat. I always put time and effort into getting a suitable gift for the person whose name I've picked, but for several years the gifts I've been given have been totally thoughtless. Last year, for instance, someone gave me earrings for pierced ears—although my ears are not pierced. I would like to pull out of the event this year. Any ideas how I can politely do this?

GENTLE READER:

There are actually two polite methods, but one of them requires a lot of effort, Miss Manners is afraid.

That one is to express gentle concern around the office about whether this sweet little holiday ruse (which unaccountably spread from dormitory life into the adult working world) isn't something of a burden on your colleagues. It's not that you find it so; everyone knows how you enjoy choosing what you give. But what about all those people who are strapped for both money and time, especially around the holidays?

Don't they have pressing enough personal holiday obligations without having to incur more at work? Doesn't everyone agree that for their sake, this should be dropped as an office activity, although of course people who have become friends on the job may still want to exchange presents on their own time?

Miss Manners happens to be one of the few people who openly denounces pseudo-social obligations at work as a nuisance. Everybody else is afraid of sounding petty or mean. But notice that she has kindly given you a way of objecting that does not sound petty or mean.

Killing the custom is the definitive solution to your problem. But Miss Manners understands it is not the solution you really want. You did throw yourself into that little game, and what you really want is a way to make others do so.

Unfortunately, that is not the other polite solution Miss Manners is offering. Hers is to put any such idea out of your head. Whoever gave you the earrings is one of those people who does not consider it a job requirement to give personal attention to a colleague—and a good thing, too, Miss Manners believes. How would you like to discover that you had accepted a personal item from the office creep who always tries to get too close to you by the printer?

So if you don't want to organize the office to get rid of the practice, just rid yourself of the notion that you should have a secret benefactor observing your earlobes while you're working and graciously accept whatever is offered without giving it undue scrutiny. But perhaps you will find that way even harder.

Paying Up

DEAR MISS MANNERS:

My workplace is a very fast assembly line, and a woman I work with came up to me while I was working and asked that I donate $15 specifically for the purchase of wedding rings for a couple at work.

The couple to be married are only acquaintances, and I was not even invited to the wedding. In addition, with their combined income, no children, and no mortgage I would think that they could afford their own wedding rings. (The total amount was $450.)

I find it impolite and unholy to ask fellow employees to pay for a gift that should come from your own heart. Consequently, I declined. I regularly give to charities, and even buy things I don't want when they're sold for a cause; and I donate to work gifts for baby showers, weddings, and deaths in the family. Was I correct in declining to donate to this particular cause?

GENTLE READER:

What? You're not willing to buy your colleagues their wedding rings? Have you no heart?

By Miss Manners' reckoning, the office is skimping on the stones. Since plain gold rings cost considerably less than $450, your coworkers must have decided that they should be treated to something fancier, but the amount is inadequate for anything substantial in the way of diamonds. Why don't you organize a major fundraising drive?

Or better yet, why don't you learn to say a polite "No" to outrageous requests: "I appreciate the opportunity, but I already give to the needy."

DEAR MISS MANNERS:

When I joined the managerial staff in a medium-sized company, my boss explained his holiday "tradition" of having each of us contribute $75 to a holiday gathering for all departmental employees and their spouses. My colleagues, having been through this before, all got out their checkbooks and reflexively handed over the money, planning to write it off on next year's taxes as "professional dues."

I wanted to find out more. When I asked how this kitty would be spent, I learned that we would be gathering at the home of another employee, that trays of various finger foods would be purchased from a local supermarket, and that the rest would be spent on wine and beer ("Good beer, ya know, good beer") and a maid service to clean up the host's home after the party (despite the fact that a sign-up sheet to do this had been posted at work and at least three employees had volunteered).

Miss Manners, I don't mind forking over five or ten dollars to help with a holiday spread at the office, but for $75, I expect something like a catered buffet and live entertainment. Moreover, I don't feel that I owe the department a holiday party, and I think that a lot of money is being wasted here. I don't know several of the employees who work evenings and nights, and I haven't even met some of them. I feel that my boss is using his status to extort money from his subordinates to host HIS party. If he wants to do so, I say let him pay for it.

When I gave my boss my regrets that I wouldn't be able to attend the gathering, he replied, "Well, in past years, even if somebody couldn't come, they paid anyway." I am not a freeloader and I indeed did not attend, but my boss just asked me for the second time since the party when I would be paying my share, and I am furious.

GENTLE READER:

Miss Manners hates to rush the season, but it's time to get ready for next year's party.

See if you can build an informal consensus, not only of managers but among the staff, for giving everyone an afternoon off in honor of the holiday, instead of a party that intrudes on time they might otherwise spend with their families and friends. You may need to show your good faith by paying this year's blackmail, but it will be worth it. You would be doing everyone a favor.

However, it might be enough just to tell your boss your plan to find out whether this might work better. As he realizes that the cost of time off will come from the business itself, he may be very ready to tell you to forget about the $75.

DEAR MISS MANNERS:

My husband and I were invited to a party to celebrate the anniversary of his boss's appointment to his present position. Each invitee was asked to pay $30 per person to cover the expense of the evening, including the meal, tax, gratuity, and a gift as a token of our appreciation for his work.

The event was two months ago. Now we have received a letter asking for an additional $20 per person to cover "additional" expenses incurred. It was stated that the planning committee underestimated the cost and "forgot" to include tax and gratuity.

Am I now responsible for the miscalculations of the committee? My husband and I would not have attended if we had known it would cost $100. The money is due soon.

GENTLE READER:

Wow, what a celebration. Your husband's coworkers must really love their boss to rush to whoop it up over his good fortune out of your own obviously much more modest salaries.

Is it possible that he really thinks so? Or that he has allowed others to talk him into believing this and authorizing them to use his name in this fashion? Then it is time to disabuse him—before the next payment.

Bear in mind that it is the office's pseudo-social presumption that is your target here, not the committee's accounting practices.

If all of you get together on this, it will be easier to avoid individual consequences. Write the boss a cheerful letter explaining that, as he knows, your salaries are not at the level where you don't have to worry about budgeting, and that, as much as you wish him well on his anniversary, you cannot afford to indulge in this celebration. Perhaps raises would be in order, you should suggest, or just special expense accounts so that you can continue to attend his parties.

CHAPTER 13

My Other Family

"Please don't disturb people. They're trying to work."

"I'll be at the desk entertaining myself."

"Would you photocopy these and distribute them to everyone?"

If these statements are made, respectively, by 1) an embarrassed employee to the child whose babysitter cancelled at the last moment, 2) the child who will therefore be spending a day at Mama's or Papa's office, and 3) Mama's or Papa's employer, then everyone is doing his or her best to handle a sometimes unavoidable inconvenience.

Unfortunately, the speakers more often appear in a different order: 1) the boss who has been cast as unfeeling when he only wants his employees to do their jobs; 2) the parent who is content to dump the child-rearing duties on his coworkers—so much the better if he assumes that this is a job for the junior, female employees—and 3) the child herself, who is ready and eager to take charge of the office.

Miss Manners is aware that her preferred scenario assumes that the child is able to exercise reasonable restraint and judgment (the parent and employer, too, for that matter). She thought she could take it for granted that infants and toddlers, at least, were not in a position to make material contributions in the office. Their skills—rolling over, grabbing an extended finger, and needing to be sanitized—although impressive, tend to be taken for granted among professional staff. Employees who stagger around the office during business hours grabbing onto things or babbling in a high-pitched voice are not generally in high demand. Those who do so after hours often discover that the fun they had at the office party is somewhat tempered by the next-day reaction of colleagues.

Flyby children—those accompanied by an unengaged parent and shown off during lunch or at the end of the day—are, by definition, adorable. And the employer who insists on throwing office parties has only himself to blame. For extended visits during work hours, children, if allowed in the office, should be neither seen nor heard.

Those who wish to complain that, my goodness, someone needs to look after the child, you cannot just ignore her . . . she is a person with needs . . . someone has to be responsible for her . . . it is heartless . . . do you know what childcare costs and . . .

What's that you say? Sorry, Miss Manners was having too much fun letting your children play with her cell phone to attend to her job, and finish stating her position.

It is more extreme than yours—and less.

More, in that she condemns the entire working structure of the society. When the professional world finally undid the impractical, as well as unfair, practice of expecting a whole gender to be the full-time domestic support staff for the working force, it quit before completing the job. The domestic part of civilized life has been therefore left woefully understaffed. Perhaps some day another obvious discovery will be made: that society has a crucial interest in the welfare of children, and therefore in making good care available, and therefore in designing respected and economically feasible jobs for parents, adult children, and professional assistants alike.

But less, in that she does not condone using the parental plight, with which she is highly sympathetic, to suspend the decorum of the workplace.

DEAR MISS MANNERS:

What to do! While I would never dream of taking children with me to a doctor's appointment or worse yet to a bikini waxing, I am faced at least once per week with the challenge of handling mothers who do. My staff has tried emailing our spa guests a polite reminder that we cannot accommodate children, only to have the same people violate this rule. They become extremely offended when, upon arriving with child (children!) in tow, they are informed that we will have to reschedule them to a time when they have appropriate childcare. If we allow the children to stay, they inevitably disturb the Zen-like environment, and we are faced with the complaints of our other guests. Help!

GENTLE READER:

Miss Manners is the last person to recommend offending customers, or anyone else for that matter. But if your customers knowingly break your rules, your choice is to revoke the rules and lose the customers who enjoy the child-free atmosphere or let the offending customers go elsewhere.

She would only caution you to take a sympathetic tone when enforcing this policy. You do not want to get into a discussion about the expense and unreliability of childcare. It would be advisable to telephone known offenders the day before an appointment—not everyone checks email regularly or thoroughly—and ask if the appointment is still convenient to their childcare arrangements, or whether they want to reschedule for another day.

Showing

DEAR MISS MANNERS:

An employee presents at least some indications of being pregnant. None of my business? Not at the moment, I'll concede that much.

But how about her coworkers? Do they have a right to know? Is there a polite way for either a boss or a fellow staffer (probably a female—I'm guessing guys best keep mum) to inquire as to whether a woman is in a condition that is certain to affect—if only to interrupt for a day or two—her job performance?

It isn't relevant to the general question, but a childless employee here has made it known that bearing offspring is in the plan on a semi-regular basis, and she looks (it's the consensus that's talking) to be about four months pregnant. According to some analysts, she even dresses the part.

GENTLE READER:

Everybody in the office is obviously having such a good time around the coffee pot—make that everybody with one exception—that Miss Manners hates to spoil the fun. But she must remind your office analysts of certain variables and uncertainties:

Not everybody who voices a desire to have children gets pregnant. Plans to have semi-regular children (with the intention, Miss Manners hopes, of regularizing them) are notoriously subject to chance and change. Not everyone who develops something of a tummy is pregnant. Every loose dress is not a maternity dress. And some pregnancies are blessedly free of symptoms that require missing work prior to the birth.

Therefore, the only way to satisfy everyone's curiosity is to wait for the lady in question to volunteer this information. If she really is four months pregnant, you probably don't have long to wait.

Miss Manners thinks it entirely possible that you are mistaken. She wouldn't have thought that a lady who announces an intention of getting pregnant, which is not on the approved list of conventional social announcements, would be shy about announcing success. But she could have her reasons. Perhaps she, like Miss Manners, has picked up on your subtext—the unpleasant suggestion that being pregnant is an imposition on one's coworkers.

A pregnancy becomes office business when it seriously affects the work schedule—"seriously" meaning more than the occasional sick day that an office is routinely equipped to handle. However interested the coworkers may be, it is not they but their supervisor who needs to know, in order to make arrangements to cover long absences, including maternity leave.

DEAR MISS MANNERS:

I recently had a baby and have been at work for a few months now since my maternity leave is finished. I have made the commitment to our baby to breastfeed. While at work, I pump my milk with a breast pump about twice a day in a secluded room tucked inside the women's restroom set aside for nursing mothers who are still breastfeeding.

There have been many situations where I will be walking down the hall with my breast pump in hand and someone will say, "Hi, Allison. Where are you going?" What is the most appropriate way to respond to this question?

It is not that I am embarrassed or ashamed of breastfeeding or pumping my milk, but I do feel that some people would rather not hear my response stated in such a way. In order to be sensitive to people's feelings, oftentimes I reply by saying "to the nursing room" or I will simply point to my pump and they will kind of get the idea. There are cases, though, where people do not get the idea after I have said and done the aforementioned and I will say, "I have to pump."

The quick response from those people is a "Yuck!" or "Ewww . . . don't tell me that." What is the most appropriate way to respond to people when they ask me where I am going?

GENTLE READER:

Is there not enough work to do in your office that people are asking those on the way to the restroom what they are going to do there?

At any rate, Miss Manners does not consider this a question that requires full disclosure. One reply of "As you can see, I'm going to the restroom" should be enough. Or, if you are feeling chatty, "I'm going to see about my baby's lunch."

DEAR MISS MANNERS:

My son, a senior in high school, has been visiting my workplace since he was in fifth grade. I need to know what to do about graduation announcements for coworkers. Yes, no, or maybe? I don't want anyone to feel pressured to give a gift; nor do I want them to feel slighted.

GENTLE READER:

Why people find it so hard to grasp that the purpose of announcements is to announce, Miss Manners has never understood. The name does provide a clue.

Announcements are not notifications of presents due, but neither are they party favors for those not invited to the party. Their job is to announce events to people who would be interested, but not otherwise aware of them.

Miss Manners would be surprised if your coworkers had not heard that your son will be graduating from high school. If he didn't go bouncing around the office exclaiming it, surely you let it slip. So they don't need announcements.

What they might like—presuming your son didn't drive them crazy and that they took a benevolent interest in him—is the opportunity to say, "It's hard to imagine you're that grown up already." He could provide this by visiting the office one more time to thank people for having put up with him and tell them that he will miss them.

Telling

DEAR MISS MANNERS:

I don't have children, but a number of my coworkers do. I would like to state that, for the record, I find children adorable and have no problem with my coworkers going on about the part little Johnny got in the school play and the like.

My problem is when they start getting into the more graphic details about little Johnny's bodily functions. Such as how little Johnny caught the flu the other day and puked all over the floor multiple times. Or how little Timmy had such bad diarrhea that it came out of both sides of his diaper. I wish I could say I was exaggerating when I recall such stories, but sadly I am not. These adults would never think to say such things about themselves but have no qualms about divulging this information when it comes to their children.

What's worse is, it seems to be contagious. One person starts a story and inevitably everyone who has kids chimes in with tales of a similar situation. This has happened so many times and with multiple coworkers that I'm beginning to think it's now the norm among childrearing adults. In addition to finding the topic of their conversation disgusting, I think it infringes on their child's privacy.

I certainly wouldn't want anyone with the intimate details of my digestive system telling gross stories about me to a group of coworkers! During these conversations I have sworn silently that when I have children I will be very conscious only to discuss relevant bodily functions with necessary parties, like their pediatrician.

In the meantime, is there anything I can do to put a stop to this topic of conversation? I don't want my coworkers to think I'm being insensitive about their children but I also don't want to be subjected to these unpleasant stories during meetings and lunches. Unfortunately, sometimes leaving the room is not an option.

GENTLE READER:

Many organizations have discovered a niche market in throwing together groups of new parents precisely to have the discussions you have observed at work. It may be endearing in the abstract that otherwise sane adults are so attached to their offspring, but in the specific it is, as you have also observed, not so charming. Miss Manners suggests you find the names of a few groups in your area, and enthusiastically inject them into the conversation. After that, if no one takes the hint, feel free to change the subject.

DEAR MISS MANNERS:

I have had the great pleasure of sponsoring a child overseas, as a foster parent. When I received a photo of the child, I was anxious to share my excitement with my coworkers at our regular lunchtime get-together.

After a brief glance at the picture, they unanimously changed the subject. It occurred to me that it may be a modern gaffe to produce a picture of poverty at the dining table. Perhaps other people's children (whether natural or fostered) are truly a social bore. Can you help me understand why this episode felt so awkward?

GENTLE READER:

Miss Manners can see that you are trying to work yourself into a funk about the callousness of the world and its indifference to poverty, children, and, especially, the combination of the two. She trusts, however, that you will not resist her attempt to head this off. It is too sad an occupation for someone of your generous spirit.

The fact is that office workers, no matter how superficially chatty and friendly, have a limited interest in the unknown families of their colleagues. Unless there are genuine, out-of the-office friendships as well, they regard these characters in the reports of their coworkers as shadowy figures. Once they heard the news and duly admired the picture, they had demonstrated the minimal interest politeness requires.

If you want to taste the joy of sharing your fortunes with others, you need friends or relations—the kind of people whose children, Miss Manners trusts, are of deep interest to you.

DEAR MISS MANNERS:

As a single adult female who is childless by choice, I am becoming increasingly annoyed with my coworkers when they interrupt my duties or free time with stories about their children or grandchildren.

I work in a close-knit atmosphere, truly enjoy my work, and get along with my boss and coworkers. I have a full social life, a partner, a home, and travel. Adult conversations are more interesting to me.

So many parents seem to live vicariously through their children and readily share all information about them with others. That's fine, but I'm just not interested. Please tell parents to respect their single coworkers' privacy by not sharing their baby's, children's, and/or grandchildren's every move or activity. I don't care to know, don't want to know. That's why I don't have children. Just because their children are cute and exciting to them does not mean they are to others. How do I solve this problem without hurting feelings?

GENTLE READER:

By learning a few polite phrases, none of which is "I have a full life without children so stop boring me with yours."

Miss Manners suggests "Oh, how nice" in an even tone with a distracted look and a vague smile that announces that your mind is on your work. While it is rude to seem too bored, it is not rude to seem too busy.

Child's Work

DEAR MISS MANNERS:

Daughters throughout the land (including my own daughter) are selling cookies to benefit their youth organizations. A coworker of mine has sent an email to all the people we work with reminding them that she's selling cookies for her daughter. So I did a "reply all" saying, "Hey me too!" People are putting up signs in the hallway directing coworkers to their cubes: COOKIES THIS WAY—>

Is this proper behavior? Less aggressive parents get fewer sales and their daughters earn fewer points. In general, the whole competitive nature of the enterprise bothers me. Also, what is the proper behavior for a person who has two or more coworkers selling cookies? Does he need to buy from all? I anxiously await your response so that I can decide whether or not to take down my 10-foot-wide sign.

GENTLE READER:

Miss Manners has a matter of some anxiety for you, as well:

Why do you want your daughter in this organization? To learn responsibility and enterprise? If so, she supposes that you can call it a qualified success. The daughters are certainly enterprising enough to get others to take over their responsibilities.

However, you are inquiring about the responsibilities of office workers and what limits these might set on their own enterprise. And a very proper inquiry it is, too.

There is, of course, that matter of what one does with one's own job while pursuing the cookie-selling trade, but Miss Manners will do you the honor of assuming that you are observing work ethics. What is in question here is observing work etiquette.

Professional behavior does not permit using embarrassment as a sales technique—and this is true of the cookie-selling profession as well as of whatever else it is that you do. Coworkers should not feel obligated to buy something they might not really want just as a demonstration of workplace cordiality. Nor does it permit personal use of common workspace, such as putting up 10-foot signs.

However—if you can sell cookies within those limits, Miss Manners will give you a merit badge. Just don't pass it on to your daughter, who hasn't earned it.

DEAR MISS MANNERS:

I work with my father at the family construction company that he started. I recently graduated from business school, and with my new outlook find that I often disagree with him on how to handle new projects and manage people. How can I discuss this with him diplomatically?

GENTLE READER:

Your father sent you to business school and took you into his company because he wanted you to give him a fresh, young point of view informed by the latest business wisdom.

So just tell him what you think. And then listen to him say, "Hey, I was running this company before you were born and I did a pretty good job of it, too, Mr. Wet-Behind-the-Ears. How do you think I paid for that fancy education of yours? And in case you hadn't noticed, I'm not quite washed up yet."

Alternatively, you can get into the habit of prefacing all your suggestions with, "I have an idea, Dad, and I'd like to know what you think of it."

Child's Play

DEAR MISS MANNERS:

My company occasionally sponsors dinner/evening/entertainment events for our staff and consultants. With 100 to 300 people in attendance, the events are held in nice restaurants, hotels, lovely rented facilities, and aboard cruising vessels.

Invitations include a spouse or a guest. Increasingly, we are asked, in the expectation that our answer is "yes," if couples might bring their infants.

Our answer is that we adore children and in fact plan other events throughout the year that include them. However, these particular events are business- rather than family-related and we could not possibly accommodate all the children our guests would wish to bring.

Usually, this is met with a disappointed attitude. What are we missing? Why would anyone want to bring a child to adult festivities or for that matter expect to bring anyone who was not invited? Is there a better way to handle the questions? And how is the situation handled if they choose to bring the child anyway?

GENTLE READER:

You are missing something really big here. Miss Manners would have thought it too big to miss, but the entire business world keeps running smack into it without noticing.

What you are missing is that this is overtime, and overtime cuts into family time.

Miss Manners realizes that you don't think of it as overtime because you have drenched it in luxury. She also realizes that you have drenched it in luxury in the hope that the employees wouldn't think of it as overtime, and thus expect to be paid in money rather than in meals. That you share the confusion you hope to create is illustrated by your referring to the event as business in one paragraph and festivities in the next.

Still, business is what it is. While the luxury may compensate some for the time, others understandably do not want to be away from their children. And that's a big enough problem without bringing up the babysitting problem this also causes. If you want to give your employees an excursion as a treat, with or without spouses and/or children, Miss Manners doesn't want to discourage you. A treat has to be really optional, however, which would not be true if one would miss a professional duty or advantage. She doesn't want to discourage you from doing business in fancy places, either, just from doing it on family time.

In any case, you must be gracious about pretending to welcome a child who is actually standing there. Tossing him overboard or in any way embarrassing him would not do. The truly gracious thing would be to take the parent out of earshot and express sympathy about the burden of parking a child during extra working time.

DEAR MISS MANNERS:

A coworker I am friendly with has a baby who is just two days older than my baby. Recently, in passing, the friend mentioned, "Oh by the way, I'll be sending out invitations for my son's first birthday, but the party falls on your son's birthday. I'm sorry, but it is the only day that I could reserve the hall. You know how our place is too small to accommodate everyone."

I appreciate the advance warning, as this is a full two months before the boys are scheduled to turn one. However, I feel that this almost preempts our plans. We weren't planning on having a large affair for our son's first birthday, but now we most assuredly cannot. We'd rather not force people to choose which party to attend (our simple backyard BBQ or her rented-hall affair).

Will this friend understand if we choose not to attend and instead spend a quiet birthday at home with our son, and are we obliged to purchase a gift?

GENTLE READER:

It would be strange if this lady did not understand that you choose to celebrate your son's birthday rather than her son's. Yet Miss Manners also considers it strange that both of you consider that a large number of your coworkers are eager to celebrate a small child's birthday.

She is assuming that the guests you and your colleague were targeting are coworkers, because of the overlap. What is generally described in privacy as "it's a bash for the kid of someone in the office—do you suppose we have to go?" is not exactly a prized ticket.

Presumably, you do not have the same relatives and intimate friends, who are the people who might be genuinely interested in the occasion. Why don't you throw your own party and invite them?

Locus Parentis

DEAR MISS MANNERS:

Although I can enjoy my friends cooing over their newborns and talking to me in baby talk, the current crop of babies at the office has been putting me, as a single person, in an awkward position. Let me give you a few examples that show the unspoken prejudice against people without children:

I explained to one coworker that even though I am single and without children, I do have a personal life that is as important to me as his personal life is to him. He acknowledged this, but in the same breath added that nothing is as important as the fact that he needed to be home promptly at the end of the day to feed his new baby. The man has a wife who is home full-time, so this is not a question of a child going hungry. What this is, is a question of my having to stay at work to complete the unfinished business of the day.

My office was having out-of-town visitors, so my supervisor asked who would be willing to take them around and entertain them for the evening. He then said he realized that people with families would be busy, so he addressed the question to me and the one other single employee. When I took a two-year transfer across the country, I had to raise a fuss to get time to make the move because I "didn't have to move a wife and kids."

Now, I am not against people having babies. And I am more than willing to cover at work for the occasional personal emergency, which can arise for anybody. However, there is a general attitude in the workplace that a person who is single should always be available because he or she can't be doing anything "really important." Well, my personal life is as "really important" to me as is a married person's to him or her.

How do I deal with this unconscious (I think it is unconscious) attitude in the office, where I will be expected to cover any extra work or emergencies that may arise? If I refuse, I am downgraded, since I obviously can't be doing anything else "really important." Meanwhile, the workers with children are not even asked to help out. I resent the inequity and I even more resent the prejudice. How can I confront this?

GENTLE READER:

You raise an extremely interesting question, and Miss Manners agrees both that there is no conscious affront intended, and that you have a justifiable complaint.

Many patterns of life in this country no longer fit the realities. For example, the discrepancy between the schoolday and the workday assumes that mothers are waiting at home to feed the children cookies, rather than out earning the money to feed them dinner.

You have run into two outmoded assumptions:

1. That workers are available for extra-hours duty because, being men, they have their domestic lives run for them by their wives, and neither have to, nor want to, participate in them.
2. That just about everybody starts out working life single, then gets married, then has children.

That the first is no longer true, you know from the attitudes of the fathers at your office. Since your office still seems to assume that there will be workers available for what sounds like more than the occasional real emergency, they have turned to you.

The second point would, if true, ensure an eventual fairness. People still in the single stage would do their extra duty knowing that when they had children, others would be along to put in their time. This ignores the fact that there are many in the workplace who will remain childless.

Miss Manners suggests that you bring the complexity of this problem out into the open. It is not a fault in a father to consider his baby to be of paramount importance; rather it is a fault in the management to consider it has the right to plunder some employees' private time.

DEAR MISS MANNERS:

I am a teacher at our church preschool. We have a large program (about 400 children, age three to five), which is subsidized by our church.

Because of the rapid growth of this popular program, we are in great need of assistance from the parents of the students. We do not want people to feel forced to help, yet we want to communicate the urgency of our need to the children's guardians. Would you help me with the phrasing of such a request?

GENTLE READER:

Miss Manners appreciates your reluctance to do what is vulgarly known as "laying a guilt trip" on those parents. She is afraid that shame and embarrassment is what most people recruiting for good causes now use, on the grounds that other people—by implication less conscientious than themselves—will not otherwise bestir themselves.

But Miss Manners cherishes the notion that you can treat grownups as adults. She therefore suggests putting the problem squarely before them: The program is overburdened and cannot successfully continue without volunteer assistance.

If you acknowledge that parents of young children are seriously overburdened themselves, you will be asking them to use their judgment to deal with a crisis you all share, rather than nudging them to do something that they have reasonable excuses to avoid.

Parentis Made Loco

DEAR MISS MANNERS:

I am a hardworking single mother with a professional career in a software company. I am accustomed to working very long hours. I have become adept at attending to my children's needs for medical appointments, school conferences, and sick days by working late into the night and early morning to compensate for any time off.

Recently I was faced with a traumatic medical emergency involving one of my children. Much to my surprise, I received mean-spirited messages from my superior, accusing me of being a part-time worker because of my responsibilities as a mother. Here is an example: "I understand that you have requirements as a mother, but we simply must have a full-time product manager."

I need to respond to these charges without being defensive about the fact that I am, in fact, a mother. What approach would you suggest?

GENTLE READER:

You can't seem defensive if you refuse to admit that you have been attacked.

You will have to steel yourself, Miss Manners realizes, to ignore that bundle of explosive emotions society keeps igniting when it should be working on a peaceful plan to allow everyone to attend to both personal and professional obligations: guilt, righteous indignation, defense of future generations, and all that sort of thing. Your boss was foolish, as well as rude, to strike that match.

But once you step away from that danger, Miss Manners hopes that you will acknowledge that he does have the authority to require you to work a full schedule, and that he may not be aware of the compensatory time you work.

All you need to do, then, is to bring this to his attention. The approach Miss Manners suggests is, "Nobody knows better than I that being product manager is a full-time job—and then some. That is why I have been working nights and coming in early, and I keep in touch on the rare occasions when I do have to be out of the office. But it's a wonderful job and I'm happy to put in the extra time."

DEAR MISS MANNERS:

My family and I have been planning a vacation in Nantucket for a week this August. I get two weeks' vacation each year so that's no problem. My dilemma is that our company has just decided to relaunch the Web site that month. Everyone in my office seems to work incredibly long hours already—even when not working on a deadline project—and few people take vacations. I feel guilty leaving during this time and am worried my boss may think I'm a slouch. On the other hand, my family is counting on me. What's the best way to take this time off and stay on the boss's good side?

GENTLE READER:

Which good side do you want to be on? The one where your boss is grateful to know that guilt works on you, making you feel you are not entitled to have a life? Or the one where he is grateful to have you, because you seem less likely to crash or quit than those whose lives are totally absorbed by work?

Miss Manners does believe it would be polite to express simple regret, to your colleagues as well as to your boss, that you will not be there during the crunch. With any luck, the project will be postponed, and you, having had your vacation, will get to do it while everyone else takes off.

DEAR MISS MANNERS:

I am a college-educated woman who works full-time along with being a full-time wife and mother of a 2-year-old. Since I worked for 10 years prior to our precious addition arriving in our lives, I have become reasonably advanced in my position and am well compensated for it. My husband and I live a comfortable, although not extravagant, life. We decided that our lifestyle and my pay were not conducive to my simply up and quitting my job upon my daughter's arrival.

Could you please advise me on how to deal with simple-minded but well-meaning acquaintances who want to sympathize with me for not being able to quit my job and stay home with my daughter? I have not complained to these people. I may have declined to join in some activities, citing spending time as a family as a reason. I want neither pity nor praise for my choices, but I also don't invite input. What can I say to these people?

GENTLE READER:

How right you are about not entering into a discussion that will lead nowhere pleasant. Miss Manners recommends interpreting such remarks as pleasantries, not as invitations to participate in the Mommy Wars, and replying, "Thank you, we're doing fine" before steering the conversation into less dangerous territory.

CHAPTER 14

Let's All Be Friends

An alarming number of people have forgotten what a friend is: A friend is a person with whom you voluntarily spend your free time because you enjoy each other's company.

Not all friendships are equal, Miss Manners acknowledges. Good friends trump those who do not rise to the level of friends-in-need (your need, not theirs). You may have longtime friends, intimate friends, and best friends, although plural forms of the latter are suspect both grammatically and dramaturgically. BFF, the "best friends forever" electronic version of an age-old aspiration, is used only by those who are neither aged nor old.

Not all friends are friends. Unless the boyfriend and the girlfriend provide more than friendliness, they are known as "just friends" or even "former friends." But particular friends and special friends may have to be seated separately at dinner if they are to be able to follow the thread of the conversation without being distracted by what is going on under the table. This is not true of anyone characterized as "an elderly friend," a phrase sometimes used as code to mean that he lost the thread of the conversation long ago. And if you find yourself addressed as "my young friend," run for cover.

Notice that the words "work," "professional," and "office" are nowhere to be found. Not being in a lawsuit with your business partner, coworker, or professional acquaintance does not make that person your friend. The assumption that at the best workplaces everyone is friends is, to Miss Manners' thinking, woefully misguided.

For starters, a friendship, like a marriage, is supposed to be a matter of mutual choice. Even if you are the boss, your association with many of the people with whom you have to work will not be voluntary, except in the limited sense that you can always quit. The President of the United States still has to work with Congress. You can, as we now say, "unfriend" an intimate who disappoints you in your private life. But unless you are a particularly active host, such a sanction does not require the erstwhile friend to find a new way of feeding himself.

That a friend is also such precisely because you are not at work is equally important. The fact that you may choose to spend your free time with coworkers is not Miss Manners' fault. Please do not complain to her about the stress of your job when you find that an evening out is spent discussing work or office politics. Perhaps your employees—I mean friends—will be more sympathetic.

None of which is to say that Miss Manners condemns all office friendships. Friendships made at work can and do exist. People who spend an inordinate amount of time together, under pressure to get things done and sharing a common purpose, may well form lasting friendships. One particularly strong form of friendship at work was recognized as early as Homer's *Iliad*, and in this case she is referring to the war buddy.

Miss Manners asks only that you make such choices consciously and recognize the pitfalls. Your war buddies are the ones who are still with you when the war is over, even if you lost—and your friends are the ones who are still with you when you leave, even if you were fired.

DEAR MISS MANNERS:

I am constantly being invited by coworkers to social gatherings after work. I usually decline. I am not a social person. After work I want to go home and veg. I hate talking on the phone, and I especially hate having guests in my home. I like most of the people I work with and don't mind lunching with them or having an occasional potluck, but after hours I like my solitude. I feel that my coworkers find me standoffish—I have heard comments from several of them. How can I make them understand that it is not personal?

GENTLE READER:

Feeling pressured into socializing with one's coworkers is a widespread problem, not a quirk betraying loneliness or insecurity. To want to decide how to spend one's own free time and with whom is surely a modest and reasonable desire.

It certainly strikes Miss Manners as more reasonable than the beliefs from which workplace social pressure arise: that to know people better always makes one fond of them; that workers who are fond of one another are more productive (when they aren't taking suspiciously long lunch hours); and that the only way to be polite is to make friends, so the choice is between snubbing one's colleagues and partying with them.

Miss Manners begs to differ. Good business manners require being cheerful, respectful, and considerate, but maintaining a professional demeanor rather than faking universal friendship. One should be able to work equally professionally with someone one can't stand and someone with whom one is madly in love, and that requires keeping some distance. When friendships happen spontaneously (as they will, and as will romances, proximity being more powerful than discretion), an extra effort at professionalism on the job is required to avoid trouble.

That trouble is most likely to arise with the assumption that coworkers have the same disinterested feelings as friends and will protect one another, as friends would, from any consequences of talking and acting freely. A sensible boss is interested in how well people work, not how enthusiastically they play.

Nevertheless, all decent invitations, even unwelcome ones, must be answered graciously. And the less specific a refusal, the more gracious it is. Even announcing that one prefers solitude sounds snobbish or sinister.

All that is necessary is to decline each invitation with thanks for being asked and regret for not being able to attend—and not to mind if one has to keep doing it or care if the invitations eventually cease. Cordiality is what is needed, not openness. Another peculiarity of the etiquette business is that we do not lightly advise people to be honest in its modern sense, because that means volunteering everything they happen to feel regardless of how hurtful it may be to others.

ANNOYING FRIENDLINESS

DEAR MISS MANNERS:

We have recently hired a new person in our office group who seems to be a charming young woman with one resounding exception. She seems to be under the delusion that TOTAL honesty is always best and anyone not agreeing is in "denial."

I already know more than I would like to of her personal life. However happy I may be for her ability to resolve her problems using "12-step groups," I can't seem to think of a polite way to indicate that the social interaction in an AA meeting should necessarily differ from that in an office. It is not always a good thing to "get everything out in the open." Have you any suggestions?

GENTLE READER:

The relevant argument here is that the worker is violating professional manners, which preclude intruding personal matters into the workplace.

Yes, yes, Miss Manners knows that you told everyone about your skiing trip, and didn't mind that a colleague ran around showing everyone pictures of his new baby. You don't want to be draconian about stamping out every pleasantry. But when personal matters become a nuisance, as they have in this case, the rule needs to be invoked.

A supervisor can do this directly, stating that the organization considers it bad professional manners. A colleague can politely refuse to participate by saying, "I'm afraid you'll have to excuse me, but I have work to do."

DEAR MISS MANNERS:

Recently I was able to locate my boss online and send an instant message saying hello. My boss was offended because he felt I had invaded his privacy. What do you think?

GENTLE READER:

That your boss does not care to have you wave at him electronically while he is working, or not working—but in any case does not care to be instantly at the call of employees. Miss Manners suggests you not break in again to apologize. The word "Sorry" on a paper memo would serve better.

DEAR MISS MANNERS:

Last night I accepted a dinner offer from a coworker. I thought we were going out just to have a pleasant meal and split the bill. As we were finishing dessert he asked if I was happy with my efforts to save for retirement. Thinking that we were still having casual conversation, I launched into the usual concerns any mid-40-year-old has . . . he then tells me the solution is to join him in this fabulous business opportunity. He hauled out the literature and made a big pitch. I felt just like one of those specimen insects pinned to parchment. How does one react to such an unwelcome advance?

GENTLE READER:

You went out to dinner with a colleague and he made you a business proposition? Quick, someone please fetch Miss Manners' smelling salts. And a lawyer, to see if this is covered under workplace harassment laws.

It is covered under social harassment etiquette, however. The rule against discussing business on social occasions will forever remain on the books, Miss Manners promises you, no matter how many people flout it. When trapped, the polite person's defense against embarrassment and boredom is to say, "Thanks, but I'm really not interested," and immediately start a different conversation.

That would have been the proper reaction here, too. Miss Manners only objects to your implication that your coworker was gauche. You thought of the evening as beginning a friendship with someone you happened to meet at work, but it was equally reasonable for him to think of it as continuing business talk off the premises.

Protective Phrases

DEAR MISS MANNERS:

I work in a small office with a extremely opinionated person. For two years now, I have listened to her opinion on everything that the present administration has said or done. These political diatribes will come out of nowhere on any given day and are always directed toward me.

As you can guess, our opinions are as different as night and day. Out of respect for our office setting and what I thought was a nice office friendship, I have tried to change the subject or make a joke of the situation. So far, I have been very proud of myself and have not lost my temper.

However, it is getting harder and harder to let these hateful remarks pass. In honesty, I am about ready to blow. Please help me with a correct and polite response that will get my point across that our views are vastly opposite and would she please keep hers to herself.

GENTLE READER:

There is a particularly irritating—but perfectly polite—phrase you must learn to repeat with a smile: "Well, we agree to disagree."

Miss Manners realizes that your officemate has entered into no such agreement, and will at first be stirred to further efforts, rather than acknowledging that nothing she says will change your mind. You will therefore have to keep claiming it over and over. But it is better than open warfare, and plastering warring campaign stickers over your respective desks.

DEAR MISS MANNERS:

In my day-to-day business, I have meetings with men who are quite a bit older than I am (I am 27). During the course of our business meetings and lunches, the same old questions arise: How far do you plan to go with your company? How long are you going to work? Do you have any children? When are you going to have children? What is a nice, pretty girl like you doing working in this business?

These questions cannot be tolerated much longer. Any suggestions you could give on politely letting my business contact know that they are embarrassing, inappropriate, and most of all none of their business, would help.

GENTLE READER:

What are such gallant gentlemen doing in business?

You might ask them that. Politely, of course, in the same tone of innocent and kindly interest as they presumably took in you. Turning questions around can never be counted as rudeness, but it alerts the original questioners that something is wrong.

Examples:

"Oh? Is there more turnover in the field than I had thought? Do you anticipate leaving your company?"

"No (or yes); do you have children?"

"Why do you ask—is your wife expecting a baby?"

Nevertheless, Miss Manners does not advise asking them how much longer they plan to work before retirement. A courteous, all-purpose answer to any employment question is "Oh, I love my job"—especially if you are angling for a better offer from the person who asked.

DEAR MISS MANNERS:

How do you behave toward a coworker who insists on—even after repeated requests not to do so—explaining in great detail what she and her husband talk about or (worse yet) do in their bedroom? Or what she and her numerous lovers have done in the past, or at the present time when her husband isn't present?

I've tried to be noncommittal in my responses, such as half-listening to her stories as I performed life-or-death clerical duties at my desk. Because we are the administrative support department, I can't always get up from my desk and walk away. Our supervisor never hears any of this, and even if she did, I don't think she would have any idea how to behave in this situation. Short of seeking employment elsewhere, what is a Gentle Reader to do?

GENTLE READER:

Miss Manners suggests that you memorize a few phrases that you can murmur absentmindedly in reply to these revelations, without regard to the particulars being dished up at the moment. This way, you do not have to take your mind off your work.

Here are some samples:

"I don't quite follow, but never mind."

"Can't you just tell your husband this yourself?"

"Why don't you send me a memo I can read later?"

"Maybe the supervisor can help you."

The supervisor has not asked for Miss Manners' assistance, but she would have an even easier time of it. The only phrase she needs to know is "Why are you discussing personal business on company time?"

DEAR MISS MANNERS:

I am a person of moderate means, quite used to socializing with peers and family both as a hostess and a guest. My husband is a construction worker. We tend to have several couples over around the fireplace or the picnic table, and are given to potluck get-togethers. It suits us fine.

I work for a man who regularly invites us to events at his home and elsewhere, where he entertains personal friends and clients at the same time. He inherited a vast amount of money, land, etc., and also made his own personal fortune in business. Our circumstances could not be more different financially or culturally.

I am in my late 30s and he is in his early 40s. I discovered that there was speculation in the office that I was hired for my looks and later earned respect for my skills from my colleagues. My employer has an attractive wife, and I am not concerned that the invitations are for any reason other than to include me in the activity.

The problem is that I prefer not to attend any of these functions. Though my boss is pleasant enough to me and we work well together as a team, I have never felt friendship for him, consider him to be arrogant and self-centered, and simply choose to keep the relationship strictly business.

I have used so many excuses (some of them were lies) that I am unhappily contemplating the next invitation. I have never attended any function at his invitation in the three years I have worked here. I tried just saying, "Oh, I'm sorry, we're busy that night." And his response is, "Oh, what are you doing?" So I lie. I've said, "Oh, isn't it funny? We're having a cookout that same day" (hoping he would note the difference between his catered cookout, where I would have to wear a dress and stockings and my husband would have to wear a suit, and our cookout with T-shirts and jeans and kids in the blow-up pool).

I don't know what to do next. Shouldn't he have already figured out that I prefer it to be business only? Isn't it a Miss Manners rule that you stop inviting a person after X refusals? I have considered saying that to him the next time (but it would take more nerve than I have and seems rude or unnecessarily rough—he is, after all, just inviting me to a fun event). I have also considered switching jobs, but I like this job and I get along well with my boss and who's to say that a new boss wouldn't present the same problem? Should I just keep on saying we aren't available and quit fretting over it?

GENTLE READER:

Certainly you should quit fretting over it. Look what you have already spun out of a simple matter of not wanting to socialize with the boss.

There are so many red herrings in your narrative—class conflict, financial rivalries, occupational and stylistic snobbery, and sexual harassment—that Miss Manners was almost disappointed to find the actual problem so simple.

Those who do not wish to accept invitations from their bosses—a wise move, in Miss Manners' opinion—need only decline. As your boss seems not to have accepted your repeated refusals (which need not have been accompanied by excuses; "I'm so sorry we can't come" is enough), you should issue a general one.

"You're very kind to keep inviting us, but our family life just doesn't permit us to socialize like that," should do it. Note that you have left open the idea that it could be anything from a heavy social schedule to domestic habits. If your boss attempts to find out, merely keep repeating, "It's so kind of you to ask us" and "I appreciate the invitations" while shaking your head regretfully.

DEAR MISS MANNERS:

The company where I work recently hired a young lady who (after requisite introductions and the passage of a few days) answered a question about stress by stating: "That's nothing. If you really want to feel stress, you should get convicted of DUI (Driving Under the Influence) like I was last year."

I replied, "Gosh, I hope you didn't kill anybody."

She became very insulted, said it wasn't THAT bad, and walked away.

How should I have responded?

GENTLE READER:

If you are under the horrified impression that you caused this social accident, Miss Manners hastens to relieve you of your remorse. You were the victim of a hit-and-run accident by someone who seems well practiced in shifting blame.

The young lady in question was careening around recklessly, tearing through what ought to have been her own privacy, when she ran into you, an innocent bystander.

That you reacted by throwing out a startled question cannot be held against you. This could be classified as rude and nosy only if it had, itself, been used to break down the decent barrier that ought to exist among professional colleagues.

HAZARDOUS FRIENDLINESS

DEAR MISS MANNERS:

I have a job that requires frequent out-of-town travel and I also work in a traditionally male field where I deal with highway engineers. Is there a polite yet firm way to buy a male colleague a drink in a bar after a long day—or accept that favor in return—and still dispel the old social baggage about further expectations? Many of these men grew up in an age when women did not buy their own drinks, even though I earn as much or more than many of them and can certainly afford it. On the other hand, many of them are likable fellows that I would enjoy chatting with over a beer after a seemingly endless series of meetings and presentations.

Do you have a suggestion of how I can express simple friendship without having a draught beer misinterpreted as a come-on, or accept a glass of white wine without feeling committed to more than interesting conversation? Please bear in mind that some of these gentlemen react to my suggestion that we split the tab as if they were wounded, so paying just for myself doesn't always work.

GENTLE READER:

Do these gentlemen always buy rounds of drinks in turn, or does their objection to paying separately apply only to you?

Miss Manners gathers that the latter is the case. If not, you could just tell the bartender ahead of time to accept payment from you for your turn, whether there are objections or not. But if so, she is afraid that you have to recognize it as a sign that your colleagues think of you as something more than a colleague. And your only hope of being collegial friends is to make them switch back from an etiquette system appropriate to gentlemen courting ladies to one that befits non-romantic working friends. The wounds they get if you pay will be scratches compared to the wound of sponsoring overtures that go nowhere.

Do this by bringing along a male friend one time—but not, as you are wrongly anticipating, a romantic friend or one who would be willing to pass for one to establish that you are not available. On the contrary, you need to demonstrate that your friendships cross gender lines.

Tell your friend to override objections by saying, "No, no, this isn't a date—let her pay or you'll spoil things for me." This won't stop them from thinking he's an admirer, because their minds are set that way; they'll just think he's an ungentlemanly one and warn you later to drop him. But that will give you a chance, in defending him, to explain the difference between friendship and courtship practices.

DEAR MISS MANNERS:

In my place of employment, I started out at the ground level. I've been there for just short of five years. Most of the other associates that are working at the ground level have been there for a while—much longer than I. When I first started I became really good friends with a man and then later with his wife and children. About a year ago, I was promoted to supervisor in charge of all the good folks that worked with me. Now most of them cooperate and are very good employees and remain my friends. But the gentleman that had become my dearest friend has become a nightmare associate. Though outside of work he and his family are loving and caring, at work he is a rogue with the attitude that because we are friends, he is protected.

From what I can see, this can only result in either me looking bad before the other associates and upper management or in the loss of a friend. How can I gain control at work of this rogue friend and maintain the friendship? Please help me out of this bewildering situation.

GENTLE READER:

Is everyone else as grateful as Miss Manners that this is not an office romance? Nobody wants to antagonize a friend by insisting that he stop presuming on the personal connection, but how much more wrenching and disillusioning it would be to be in love with someone who put one in this position.

The simplest solution would be to recuse yourself from supervising your friend. You would tell management that as you are a close friend of his family's, you should not be the person to oversee his work, and then let him take his chances with whomever else they assign.

But perhaps this is only the simplest solution for Miss Manners. You may have reason to suspect that far from admiring how ethical you are, your own supervisors would consider this an inconvenience, even an annoyance, that lessens your own usefulness in the company.

The alternative is to demonstrate to your friend by your manner that you have two distinct relationships with him and do not consider that they overlap. In your professional capacity, you should call him to task on his job performance in a formal manner. But to emphasize your desire to maintain the friendship, you could do it when you know you will also soon be meeting him socially, at which time you should be brimming with friendliness—but careful to deflect any attempts to discuss work with the airy observation that you want to forget that and enjoy his company.

If this doesn't work—if he carries his upset over your professional criticism into your social life—you will unfortunately know that you cannot continue to be such friends. This will not be so much because it might endanger your job, as because you will know that he is not up to having a disinterested friendship. And be grateful that you are not in love with him.

DEAR MISS MANNERS:

I am beside myself in hurt and anger. I recently formed friendships at work with the women in my department (Friends A) and a woman in another department (Friend B). We enjoyed exchanging gifts at work. It was warm and fuzzy.

One day, we all came to work, myself arriving shortly after the others. I didn't expect to see Friend B because I knew she'd be working on a project in another part of the building. Shortly into the morning, noting that a key employee (X) was absent, I asked one of the Friends A if management was going to pull Friend B from her project to fill in for X. Her response was, "Oh, you didn't know? Her mother had a heart attack and B won't be here today. So-and-so told me this morning."

Miss Manners, I was very hurt that not one of "Friends" A thought to tell me this tragic news about "our" Friend B when I first came to work and greeted them. Am I wrong to feel this way? I can't help feeling betrayed.

GENTLE READER:

Your friend's mother had a heart attack, and your reaction was to feel hurt, angry, and betrayed?

Did Miss Manners miss the part where you rushed off to offer your sympathy and assistance to Friend B and, only after the situation was stabilized, began to reflect that you could have been of more help if you had been told earlier?

Miss Manners certainly hopes so. She would hate to think that such tragic emotions as you describe were aroused by feeling left out of the gossip loop at a time when a friend would be too overcome with sympathy to think about herself.

DEAR MISS MANNERS:

Two people where I work were recently accused of very serious embezzlement charges a few weeks before another coworker's wedding. Is there any situation where it is acceptable to withdraw an invitation to an event because of misdeeds of an invitee, either publicly accused or publicly convicted?

The two people accused were escorted out of the building in the middle of the workday and immediately became nonentities, reminiscent of the book *1984*. They'd already been invited, and accepted, invitations to a coworker's wedding. If I'd been the bride, I would have assumed that they would be no-shows. However, one of the two did show up, creating an extremely awkward situation for everyone.

Other than possibly asking, "So, what have you been doing for the last few weeks while the company decides whether or not to press felony charges?" no one knew what to say.

All things considered, it was not all that big a deal, although the bride and many guests were made to feel uncomfortable on what should have been the bride's day.

However, I'd imagine that there have been worse cases, such as people being publicly charged and/or convicted of child molesting or sexual assault in the time between invitations going out and an event occurring. I guess if the situation were bad enough, one could always cancel a party but cancel a wedding? What's a bride to do?

GENTLE READER:

Get married in the presence of those with whom she wanted to share the occasion only a few weeks ago. Miss Manners knows of no exemption granted to brides in the matter of believing the accused to be innocent until proven guilty. If they have been convicted, the state will usually take responsibility for them. Otherwise, this is an opportunity to demonstrate one's loyalty to one's friends. And please don't tell Miss Manners that these are not friends, just coworkers whose characters are totally unknown to the bride. In that case, they should never have been invited to the wedding.

HAZARDOUS INTERFERENCE

DEAR MISS MANNERS:

I have 8 male law partners. At least once a week some or all of us go out for lunch or a drink after work. We have at least two scheduled partner retreats a year during which we go out of town to meet and work on business plans. This has never been a problem in the past even though I am not married and seven of the eight others are.

Now we have welcomed a new partner into our group, and his wife, without coming right out and saying so, has made it very clear that she resents my presence at the otherwise "all male" outings. Should I try to smooth over this situation or leave it to the husband and wife to sort it out on their own?

GENTLE READER:

That the wife is insulting your new partner by insinuating that he cannot be trusted not to go after you is not your business. That she is insulting you by insinuating that you might go after him is.

Miss Manners suggests smoking this out by remarking regretfully to him that his wife does not seem to like you, and that you hope you did not inadvertently offend her. If he is as smart as you must have thought when taking him in as a partner, he will deny this and go home and tell her to behave herself. Should he be so foolish as to admit her jealousy, he needs an orientation talk about the cordial professionalism that is expected of everyone at the firm and, by extension, anyone a partner may bring to a firm event. You may want to ask one of the most senior partners to deliver this.

CHAPTER 15

More Than Friends

It has come to Miss Manners' attention that while everyone who falls in—or out—of love has written a song about it, there are fewer songs about employment. She has a theory about this.

Love is a good topic because of the range of emotions it inspires. It is easy to see how newfound love can inspire a celestial aria like Giuseppe Verdi's "Celeste Aida." Or how the death of a loved one can cause a Richard Wagner heroine to die sympathetically. (See act three of the composer's operatic attempt to prove that Tristan and Isolde are meant to be together, despite five hours of fairly clear evidence to the contrary.)

Employees driven to sing are, as a rule, merely disgruntled. Gruntle or, more accurately, the lack of it, does not inspire such beauty. Even Snow White's seven dwarves are not as elated by the diamonds they "dig up by the score" as by the fact that they are going home. Heigh ho.

Whether or not Miss Manners is right that wages, hours, and working conditions do not make the best song topics, if you fall in love at the office, don't sing about it. Getting work done requires a level of concentration, and usually a suspension of emotion, which are not characteristic of a great romance. Or, for that matter, of a great tenor.

In addition to the emotional conflict between love and work, there is a nearly irreconcilable conflict between their respective etiquette systems. Each system imposes its own hierarchy and they do not mix.

Miss Manners' letter bag is stuffed with complaints about the interference of the boss's wife in the office. (It is always the wife—bosses' husbands are either more discreet, less interested, or better trained.) The letters come from the boss's employees, who suffer the negative aspects of that marital bond without, one assumes, the benefits. Miss Manners supposes that bosses in this position are aware of the downside and struggle with it, but have decided that it is less life-threatening to be in trouble at work than at home. That is not a help to the employees.

Office affairs are even more pernicious. They may be good fodder for gossip, but they are bad for business, giving unsatisfied employees a new means of redress for unrelated complaints.

If the coworker romance is bad enough, romance in the chain of command carries its own special pain. Because she has less artillery than the US Army, Miss Manners does not assert a ban on romantic entanglements in the workplace, but she is sympathetic to the employees who wonder if favoritism is not being shown in these cases when it comes to hiring, firing, promotion—and other business rewards. To borrow a business phrase, caveat emptor.

Worse still is the office romance that dissipates—or explodes—and tends to do so with alarming frequency all over the conference table. It is followed by days, months, or years of reestablishing a working relationship, since never seeing the other person again carries with it a high cost, namely changing jobs. Office romances, if unavoidable, should be kept off the premises, and not just "to the extent possible," as she has noticed that people in love tend to make up their own sense of the possible.

It is in vain, Miss Manners supposes, for her to point out that the above dangers are one more good reason to get out of the office occasionally, her simplistic answer to the justification of participants that work is the only place they meet people. Nor to add that the gentleman who was working on the railroad just to pass the time away also discovered the cost of spending too much time on the job. Someone's makin' love to Dinah, which he infers from the fact that love is the only thing that could be more interesting than playing the banjo.

If You Must

DEAR MISS MANNERS:

I am a 23-year-old single male. There is a young woman (24) at work. She is so sweet, and has the name to go with it, also has a really sweet voice to go with it.

I am almost sure she doesn't have a boyfriend as I asked her what she did for the weekend recently, and she said she cleaned her room. Also I am almost sure that she doesn't smoke or drink. Neither do I. About the only thing I know about her is that she has two brothers and one sister. I know she is the oldest child in her family, because she told me.

I would like to ask her out on a date, spend the rest of my life with her, and have a family with her. That is how much I like her. I don't know how to ask her out on a date, as I have never had a girlfriend. Someone at work told me it is not a good idea to date a person from work, but I like her so much.

I talk to her every day at work but not face to face, as she is on the help line. I feel if I don't ask her out I never will find another person so pretty and sweet. I know my parents would accept her, as my parents frequently ask if I have any girlfriends, and the response has always been no. This person is so down-to-earth, I think we would make a great couple. Could you please advise me on what to do?

GENTLE READER:

Well, young gentleman, the first thing to do is to get a grip on yourself. Charmed as Miss Manners is by your outpouring, it certainly does reinforce your admission that you do not know how to ask a lady out for a date.

This sweet young thing, with her sweet name and sweet voice, may believe in true love at first sight and dream that a nice young man like you will come along and sweep her off her feet. Nevertheless, if you let on that although you know nothing much about her, you would like to have a family with her, she will scream and run. Or haul off and smack you. Or report you to your supervisor. Sweet young things have to protect themselves. You should listen to the person who told you that it is not a good idea to date at work.

No, wait! Do not despair. Miss Manners only said that you should listen, not that you should give up hope of ever dating this young lady. Although your informant is right, she is soft-hearted enough (Miss Manners, that is—we don't yet know how soft-hearted the sweet young thing may prove to be) to hope that this will be the exceptional romance that will turn out to be more important than the job.

Fortunately for you, the approaches to courtship and work-related comradeship are similar. You need to establish a collegial bond with this young lady before you can hope for a non-work friendship. Oddly enough, it is more flattering for a lady to have a casual acquaintance pounce on her opinions than on the idea of making her the smoke-free mother of his children.

So you need to pay attention to whether or not she encourages you before you propose—no, not marriage, but a cup of coffee that, if successful, might lead to a date. Without encouragement, you risk being a pest—which may be bad for the job but is certain death for romance.

DEAR MISS MANNERS:

How could I tell my boss that she is a wonderful person? I've been wanting to tell her this before, but I feel she might take it wrong. She is caring, understanding, and thoughtful. She is vice president of the corporation. She has treated me with respect since day one, and has always been a lady.

How could I tell her that she is so elegant, with class, a real lady, that she reminds me of Claudette Colbert? That's how beautiful she is.

She is smart, tough, strong, and at the same time loving. In our department, three of us work for her, one white, one black, and one Hispanic (me). I feel like we are her rainbow tribe. She makes us all feel and know that we are a team. Do you think that is laying the sugar on too heavy? Oh, she also has the most caring eyes and soft-speaking voice. She's no wimp, either. She can be stern.

GENTLE READER:

Miss Manners is glad you recognize that one can be both caring and stern, because that is what she is about to be with you.

It is wonderful that you admire your boss, and that you want to tell her so. But do not attempt to do this until you have mastered the difference between professional and personal compliments.

The effect you want in return is "How nice to be appreciated—and what a wonderful employee he is," not "Uh-oh, problem." In the meantime, Miss Manners insists that you learn to clothe your ardor in professionalism. The paragraph about the lady being understanding and thoughtful is fine. The next one is decidedly not. The part about the team is fine; the part about her eyes is not.

DEAR MISS MANNERS:

I am single at 39, and I work at a music store where most of the employees are 19 to 22. It is very hard to meet people in their 30s or younger that I'm attracted to. My problem is I meet many interesting people while I'm working, but don't know how to approach them, without seeming tacky or overbearing, while on the job. Is there a tactful way of asking someone for their number or out without offending them?

GENTLE READER:

You do know, Miss Manners trusts, that you are not supposed to be hitting on people connected with your work—either colleagues or customers? So what you really want to know is how to do this without getting into trouble.

Fortunately the polite way is also the safest way, and may even be the most effective. (Or may not. Love being bizarre, Miss Manners is aware that bold rudeness is also appreciated by people who come to hate it if their love affairs are successful.)

That is to start an interesting conversation related to the business at hand, which should be particularly easy in a music store. All you have to do is talk about the music. Then, just when the conversation is getting interesting, you break it off, saying, "I'd love to talk more to you about this. Would you like to meet for coffee after work?"

Such an invitation is purposely devoid of romance or pressure, and can be easily refused. But if it is accepted, you get the person off the premises—and away from work restrictions to the merely normal social ones.

Saying No

DEAR MISS MANNERS:

I am a doctor and a female patient has written a note to me clearly suggesting she would like to enjoy a social relationship with me. While flattered, I cannot do this. Please advise me how I can let her know this in the most gracious, kind, professional manner . . . short of telling her I am gay.

GENTLE READER:

Have you thought of confessing that you have professional ethics and therefore don't date patients? Miss Manners doesn't want to push you into revealing anything you would rather keep secret, such as an adherence to the standards of your profession, but this does seem to her a bit short of telling her about your sex life.

DEAR MISS MANNERS:

I find myself in a prickly situation involving that etiquette bugaboo, office romance. I work in an office staffed largely by young, unmarried people, where one might expect to encounter blossoming romances at every turn. Indeed, as one of the few married persons on the staff, I have observed with amusement the coffee-break courtships and after-hours dalliances. But alas, in a twist of irony, I am now enmeshed in an unrequited romance myself—a male colleague has developed a quite obvious "crush" on me.

I have tried several ploys to dissuade his interest: prominently displaying photographs of my husband on my desk; encouraging my colleague's interest in the many attractive, unmarried young women in the office; pointing out that I am several years older than he. Nevertheless, he persists.

The situation is rapidly becoming uncomfortable—for myself and for others in the office who have noticed my predicament. Because I do feel friendship and collegiality toward this young man, I do not wish to hurt or embarrass him. However, I am becoming quite desperate. How can I disengage myself from this gentleman's affection without hurting his feelings or jeopardizing our working relationship?

GENTLE READER:

No one is more admiring than Miss Manners of a desire to spare the feelings of others. But she is puzzled at your conviction that someone who refuses to stop pressing his unwanted attentions on a married coworker has such exquisitely sensitive feelings as to require being handled with extreme delicacy.

Rather, Miss Manners suspects it is exactly the delicacy of what you call your ploys that has encouraged renewed assaults on your virtue. You express friendship, not just mere office collegiality; you declare yourself charmed by the general idea of office romance, rather than considering it inappropriate to a professional atmosphere; and you base your refusals on irrelevant considerations (your age, the availability of other ladies) rather than the obvious ones.

Both as a married lady and as a colleague, you should be indignant at being solicited for romance. Miss Manners is not suggesting that you be rude about showing this, but you should be clear. Here are three clear rejections, in order of strength:

1. "Surely you can see that you are wasting your time with me. And I'm afraid your behavior is going to interfere with our pleasant working relationship."
2. "Surely you can see that I find your interest in me improper. Please don't persist, or I'm going to have to enlist help to make you stop."
3. "I believe this is what is known as sexual harassment. I will not tolerate being pestered like this, and I plan to report it."

It is Miss Manners' opinion that this person has already qualified himself for the second answer, and is rapidly approaching a need for the third.

DEAR MISS MANNERS:

I work in a somewhat casual environment, dominated by creative types including graphic designers and copywriters. It's very much a friendly team atmosphere in which people socialize both during and after hours. A few weeks ago, a fellow associate invited me to his home for chili with his wife and another couple from work. With just three months with the job and the company, I assumed the invitation was innocent and with intentions simply to "get to know the new gal" and make her feel welcome. As it turns out, however, a close friend (another fellow associate) of this inviting associate has more than a "friendly interest" (unrequited) in me and the dinner is meant to be a "set-up." Unfortunately this is to occur without my permission or approval.

Actually, it is meant to occur without even my knowledge prior to the event. But you know how word gets around. I have no interest in dating this fellow. Plain and simple. So I ask you, is this type of behavior fair? Is it socially acceptable to set a person up without telling them? Also, what should I do now? Back out of the dinner? Struggle thru it as tho nothing odd is happening?

GENTLE READER:

Miss Manners regrets to tell you that nothing odd is happening. Nothing delightful may be happening, either, and she offers you her sympathies on that, but the set-up is highly conventional.

You have not been set up for a proxy marriage, or even another date. You've only been invited to dinner, and are required to do nothing except honor your commitment by showing up and being pleasant to the other guests. It is not unfair for hosts and their friends to have romantic hopes, so long as they recognize that they may well be disappointed.

Hearing Yes

DEAR MISS MANNERS:

I work with a very good friend of mine who happens to also be a man. We often get lunch together and even split lunches to cut down on the high costs in the city. I recently found out that one of my coworkers is expressing her concern that we are involved in an affair. Having recently been married to the only man I have a relationship with, I am quite offended by such unfounded gossip! My question is this: How do

I put an end to such nonsense without creating an even bigger scene? My coworker has told senior management, so I'm afraid the problem has gotten too big to ignore.

GENTLE READER:

Doesn't anyone have any compassion for the unemployed? When the chaperonage system was abolished, on the practical grounds that besides constituting a public nuisance, it didn't even work, some highly experienced practitioners were thrown on their own resources. They are doing the best they can, running around reporting who was seen with whom, only to find, poor souls, that nobody much cares.

Miss Manners suspects this is the case here. She also suspects that the failure rate is because the chaperones are still going by the old definition by which adultery was considered proven, namely, inclination and opportunity. But as inclination is something nobody can judge for sure—most people aren't even sure of their own inclinations—they depend on the idea that there was no other reason a lady and a gentleman would want to spend time together.

Few people can still believe that. When chaperonage was discontinued, and we developed coeducational dormitories and workaholics of all genders, it became obvious that people are nowhere near as excitable as was fondly imagined. Left unsupervised, even teenaged boys and girls have been known just to rent movies and talk about how bored they are.

So while you are worried that the gossip "has gotten too big to ignore," Miss Manners is with those who tend to doubt that. Ladies used to be warned not only to behave themselves, but to curtail even innocent activities, with the threat that "people will talk." The catch is that some people will talk no matter what, so there is no point in trying to placate them. Staging some kind of display of innocence, as several people suggest, would only make things worse. When married couples make a huge show of their affection, even pure-minded Miss Manners begins to wonder.

Employer interference would, indeed, be more serious, in that it would be a serious invasion of the employee's privacy. However, there has been no sign of this. Should anyone from management dare to bring up the subject, you should react as any respectable lady should who is questioned insultingly about her private life: with outraged indignation that anyone could be so dirty-minded.

DEAR MISS MANNERS:

We discovered early this year that a former coworker had been involved in an affair with a married man whose wife had just given birth (and by just, I mean in the hours immediately before one of their dalliances). This affair continued for several months, and on more than one occasion the coworker lied about her business travel plans in order to spend time with this man, leaving her team members in the lurch.

The affair is now common knowledge and the coworker has moved on to a position with another company. Recently she returned for an office visit, and a couple of us decided to put forward a front so cold it would rival winter in the Yukon. We wanted her to realize that we are not only aware of her indiscretions, but we absolutely do not approve.

Others in the office have chastised us because they don't feel she has committed an offense since she did not sleep with their husbands. Those of us on the chilly side feel her behavior was a sign of a significant lack of character. Miss Manners, should we just overlook her behavior, as we were not personally affected?

GENTLE READER:

If people never expressed social disapproval except in cases in which they were personally involved, society would be in a bad way. And when they do, it is often in a worse way.

That is to say that social standards are maintained by a show of disapproval when violated. If there is no apparent public interest in how badly people behave, behavior in general keeps getting worse. And yet a great deal of cruelty and, indeed, outright injustice has been directed at individuals under this mandate.

That is likely why your colleagues shy away from registering disapproval. However, this does appear to Miss Manners to be a sound case. Proving affairs is dicey, even when everybody seems to know, because there are seldom eyewitnesses. But you know of her cheating on the job, and that does constitute an offense against those of you who had to fill in for her. It is also an offense against the standards of the office. A warm welcome would indeed suggest otherwise.

DEAR MISS MANNERS:

Two of my colleagues have divorced their spouses and are now dating one another. While speculation has circulated about them dating for the past year or so, one divorce just became finalized while the other one is still being completed.

While they have told a few people around the department, they have not told me personally, and while we've seen them together on our city's subway, they have not come out as an official couple.

I am very confused on how to act around them when it comes to social pleasantries. Obviously it's not polite to ask how their spouses are doing, but is it polite to ask how they are doing, or how the children are doing? Or simply leave it to how the weather is today? I do not wish to make a faux pas. At what point do the divorces become common knowledge and I should be expected to know about it?

GENTLE READER:

The number of conventional inquiries one can make without running into land mines lessens every day, Miss Manners has observed. "How are the children?" seems innocuous enough—but what if the children are siding with the deserted spouses and have stopped speaking to these ones?

"How are you?" is quite enough. Fortunately, you are not required to comment on the situation unless they bring it up, in which case you can get by with "I wish you both well."

THE BREAK-UP

DEAR MISS MANNERS:

I am the owner of a small and struggling appliance repair business. The store stays busy all the time, but we're still a long way from becoming profitable, because I only recently opened.

The lady I had been dating for the past several months naturally brings her appliances to me for repair, or I go to her house, depending on the size of the appliance. Because she was rather special to me, I never charged her for my time nor my trips, and she was always appropriately grateful and understanding enough of my situation to cover my cost on any parts involved.

But apparently I was not quite as special to her, because she decided to throttle our relationship back to a platonic level and start seeing other people. This was not a great disappointment, because there had never been any talk of love or marriage or a future together, so—friends it was.

A month later, her washing machine failed. After three hours of work, I handed her a bill. She flew into a rage because I had the nerve to charge her for my services "after we had once dated."

Is it proper for a woman to expect to pay nothing for goods and services at a business simply because she is dating—or once dated—the owner? Is it reasonable to complain about having been charged for a legitimate business expense just because there is a personal relationship? Is it logical to become offended at the idea of paying one's way while ignoring the fact that one has saved countless multiples of the expense? There must be some rules on the subject somewhere.

GENTLE READER:

Wait a second. Miss Manners is checking under both Affections and Appliances. And it seems that there is a rule under each of these headings that one should accept a favor graciously and refrain from complaining when it is removed.

You are annoyed and justly so that the removed favor aroused the lady's anger. There is no excuse for that.

However, the lady probably sees your change of policy as an expression of anger over the removal of what used to be delicately known as her favors. And while she is less justified, Miss Manners has to acknowledge that you did intend to link the two.

No one is required to provide free professional services to friends. But to make a connection between intimacies and value returned is not gentlemanly. Your change in policy should have been timed and worded so as to avoid this suggestion.

DEAR MISS MANNERS:

I had an intense friendship that bordered on the romantic with a younger colleague of my husband's. The two of them are friends, and I expect we'll meet him when we attend a conference next month. My husband may want to socialize with him. The colleague and I never acted on our feelings, and are not speaking anymore. (We used to have an extensive correspondence.)

I don't know what attitude to take with him when I see him again. It might be awkward to avoid him, since I would then be avoiding other people my husband wants me to meet, but I think it would pain me to pretend to be light and casual over drinks. It was right to stop talking to him, but I miss him very much. Then I think that if we're going to be running into him in the course of my husband's work in the future, I should get over the awkwardness now. What would you suggest?

GENTLE READER:

That you get over the awkwardness and deal with him as you would any other colleague of your husband's.

But suggesting and trusting are two different things. Why should Miss Manners trust you to be able to do this when you make it clear that you do not trust yourself?

So she is revising her suggestion. You are required to be polite to all these people you encounter, but you are not required to be equally friendly with them all. This is one person you should avoid—excusing yourself to greet others, to powder your nose—as much as you can without making it obvious to anyone except himself. Should your husband pick up on this, you should call on the privilege of having private preferences and say, "Oh, I don't know; there's just something about him—and there are so many others I'd rather talk to."

THE MARRIAGE

DEAR MISS MANNERS:

I am writing on behalf of a large group of us who work for an organization of about 60 people. We are at a loss as to how to deal with what we consider a major breach of workplace etiquette and ethics.

A married couple has been promoted to top spots. They are basically nice people—hard workers with a lot of savvy in their areas, and before their promotions they were respected for their contributions. Now they have the office in a constant uproar because they cannot seem to separate their work and personal lives.

Disrespecting the organizational chart, they extend their supervisory reach to all who work for either of them. They often give us assignments that serve their spouse's needs at the expense of our primary work. We know they exchange personnel information that should stay between a supervisor and employee.

Because they have consolidated so much power, they can push their joint agenda through during planning and budgetary sessions even though this agenda does not necessarily reflect organizational needs. They schedule unnecessary trips together, which has caused our clients to talk about the "mom and pop" nature of the organization.

We could, individually or as two separate groups, go to the supervisors to complain, but we know there will be retribution if we complain about one spouse to the other. We could go to the top boss, but he is new and seems oblivious to the situation. We think he would try to put a stop to their conduct if he were aware of it, but we do not know how that would occur without his telling these two that we have complained that they are creating an untenable situation.

There are other spouses and close relationships in the organization that have never caused similar problems, so it is not the personnel policies that are at fault—just these two.

GENTLE READER:

This is the sort of thing that gives marriage a bad name. Two people having an adulterous affair in the office would at least observe the formalities, Miss Manners dares say.

Appreciating the delicacy of your and your colleagues' position, she offers you the protection of the etiquette trade—as a cover. You have Miss Manners' permission to send the top boss a memo from the staff, saying how pleased you all are that the company is a leader in pioneering family employment. And because it is a relatively new phenomenon, you would like guidelines on managing traditional office hierarchies in such situations.

If you really want to be sneaky (although Miss Manners should choose a better word if she doesn't want to besmirch her noble profession), you should request that several couples, including the particular one you happened to mention to Miss Manners, would be eminently qualified to draw up these guidelines.

DEAR MISS MANNERS:

I am creative director of a Web site. My boss recently brought in his wife, a freelance artist, to design a section of the site. She has asked for free rein over her project, but I'm concerned that this will lead other product-line managers to want the same for their sections. The result would be a design mishmash that I believe will lead to poor sales. Given her personal connections to the top brass, how do I override her without jeopardizing my position?

GENTLE READER:

By allowing your boss the privilege of jeopardizing his. Miss Manners apologizes for scripting the instructions for accomplishing this, but she wants to make sure that you impress your boss with both your politeness and your devotion to business—even as you impale him on the professional and personal dilemma he has created.

First, you approach him with a beaming smile. A bathroom mirror rehearsal is suggested, as you must force a smile that must not look forced. "I'm delighted to be working with your wife," you say. "She's terrific." Then you turn to leave, as if you have discharged the full intent of your visit. But before exiting, you turn back and ask, "I presume you want me to treat her like everyone else?"

What is he going to say—"No"? (And if he does, you reply, "Sure, but it's going to be a sensitive issue and I don't want to upset anyone. It would be best if you issue guidelines, so everybody will understand what you want here, and not try to claim the same privileges.")

Next, you welcome the wife with that same beaming smile and a similar offhand remark: "Of course I assume you want to be treated like an artist, not like the boss's wife." You have to be sure to get this in before she outlines her plans, so that when she does, you can tell her what "all our artists" do. Then, when she insists that she has a special deal, you can say, "Oh, you'll have to take that up with my boss."

She may, and she may even win. But you will have alerted him that this would ruin office morale, and her that it would undermine her professional reputation. So instead of jeopardizing your job, you will have jeopardized only their marriage.

DEAR MISS MANNERS:

My husband and I, respectively president and owner of a business, are unsure of whom to include at our daughter's wedding. She works for us now on a part-time basis and her fiancé works for us full time.

One of us has the opinion we should put out an open invitation due to our positions. Another opinion is the bride and groom should invite only those they want to attend. We don't want hurt feelings, nor do we want anyone to feel obliged to buy a gift.

GENTLE READER:

Your position at this wedding is parents of the bride and hosts of her wedding. The guests you should invite are your and her close friends and relatives, and those of the bridegroom and his family, without regard to where these people work.

Miss Manners would hate to think of your bringing your position as employers into this purely private situation. You are acquiring a son-in-law, not extending his working hours. Anyway, inviting employees with no social ties to your family is not the way to avoid hurting their feelings. It just changes hurt at being excluded to hurt for being "expected" to attend and to send a present.

DEAR MISS MANNERS:

My husband (who is 20 yrs my senior) works with a female that is 30 yrs his jr. and they have developed a "friendship." He tells me that he thinks of her as a daughter; however, they go for a beer every night after work, and this always turns into several beers. They text each other at least 50 times a day. I have asked, to no avail, that they not text on weekends.

Every time we have a disagreement, he always compares me to her. I have asked him point-blank if he is in love with this person (who by the way is also married). He has not said yes, but he has not said no.

Am I the stupid one for wanting to fight for my husband? This woman even bought a secret phone so that they can text each other and her husband does not find out. I know in my own mind that if an affair has not yet happened it is just a matter of time. How do I know all this? They invited me to have a beer with them, then I realized I was a decoy for them. As I write this, I realize just how dumb I am to stick around.

GENTLE READER:

Glad to have been of help.

Keeping Your Hands to Yourself

DEAR MISS MANNERS:

I am a reasonably attractive, single female attorney who reluctantly finds myself at the receiving end of greeting pecks from men (and women!) with whom I would prefer to maintain a more formal relationship. A handshake is preferred.

Must I return the "favor"? May I simply present my cheek and then move to a safe distance? What does one say? How does one respond to the other men who invariably say, "He didn't kiss ME hello!"

GENTLE READER:

What about, "Yes, why don't you?"

And then stand back.

You will then have embarrassed the two gentlemen no more seriously than they have embarrassed you. And you will have made the point that kissing is a silly greeting between people who see each other professionally, where gender should not be a factor in proper professional manners. And even if you don't get the comment from a bystanding gentleman, stand back anyway at the first sign of a pucker.

You are under no obligation to accept social gestures from those whom you do not know socially, especially if they undermine your professional status by suggesting that you are there foremost as a lady and only secondarily as an attorney.

But professional manners demand of you that you not administer a public rebuff to someone who may be supposed to be simply silly, rather than evil. Thus, you should cover his confusion by smiling and putting out your hand for a proper handshake.

Happily Ever After

Congratulations. Having wisely done everything Miss Manners recommends, you have thrived in your professional life, undistracted by emotional turmoil from neglecting your personal life. So has your partner, who was reading over your shoulder. Professional setbacks were cushioned by the support of real friends, and personal problems did not also get you fired. You made time for both work and play by graciously avoiding events that were neither.

Now that you are in charge, things have gotten busier, but you are in a better position to eliminate silly pseudo-social business entertaining.

Well, not quite.

When the CEO of your new Chinese affiliate comes to town, when you host a party for the aldermen who helped you get the permits for your new building, when you sit down to a state dinner for a foreign president or monarch—you are going to have to socialize at work. Much will be said, on such occasions, about everlasting friendship. Much will be drunk. Presents may be exchanged. Hugs will almost certainly be exchanged.

But would you stand by these people if they lost their positions? Would they stand by you? Mistaking these declarations and social trappings for friendship—and an amazing number of seemingly sophisticated people do—puts you back on the level of the intern who believes the boss who said that the office party was just a chance to have fun and speak freely.

These functions are ceremonial, and the statements and gestures are symbolic—an expression of anything from active cooperation to armed détente; they are not a chance to relax. It's no use complaining that this means that they are no fun. Count your blessings that treaties are no longer formalized by having to wed your counterpart's hapless daughter.

But to maintain the fiction of friendship, you may have to bring your own spouse, and this can sow almost as much dissension as a new queen who doesn't speak the language. The "First Lady Problem," to give it a label, is not confined to the palace or the White House. It is an evolving area in business manners. For starters, the partner can now be expected to be coming straight from his own job, with his own business reception the next night at which you, in turn, will have to appear.

The potential sources of unpleasantness in this arrangement stem precisely from the blurring of the line between the personal and professional—a point that Miss Manners thinks would be familiar by now. The partner is annoyed because he considers himself a captive guest. The guests feel put out when the partner does not pay them sufficient attention. And the staff bristles at the perceived interference of a nonprofessional.

It is a no-win situation that doesn't even pay. Doing too little reflects badly on the couple, and doing too much is perceived as outrageous. Only courteous restraint by both spouse and staff can make this work—the spouse recognizing that he is not present to be entertained, but to act as co-host with the attached duties and responsibilities, and the staff recognizing that he is an honorary employee.

The compensation is that the two of you will not have neglected each other, your relatives, or your real friends. Thus you will have people with whom to joke, complain, strategize, relax, and retire happily ever after.

Index